Differentiated

SUPER
VISION

Allan A. Glatthorn

About the Author

Allan A. Glatthorn is Professor of Education at the University of Pennsylvania Graduate School of Education, where he teaches and conducts research in supervision, curriculum development, and the teaching of writing. He has been a high school teacher, department head, principal, and director of two alternative schools. He has published several English textbooks, numerous professional articles, and two monographs on the English curriculum and the teaching of writing.

Editing:
Ronald S. Brandt, *ASCD Executive Editor*
Jo Ann Irick, *Assistant Editor*

Price: $8.50
ASCD Stock Number: 611-84326
ISBN: 0-87120-124-0
Library of Congress
  Card Catalog Number: 83-73347

Contents

Foreword

Allan Glatthorn has provided us with a practical and useful guide to current practices in supervision. He certainly achieves his stated purpose—to establish a rationale for a "differentiated system" for the supervision of instruction.

Professor Glatthorn also presents a concise analysis of the key characteristics of various forms of the four approaches he espouses: clinical supervision, cooperative professional development, self-directed development, and administrative monitoring. For each approach, he furnishes a review of related research, illustrative examples, and citations of major strengths and potential weaknesses. His suggestions for implementation add an important dimension to the work. The inclusion of numerous excellent references provides the reader with the information needed to study each of the four approaches in greater detail.

The unusually fine blend of theory, research, critical analysis, and review of promising practices is in keeping with ASCD's long tradition of highlighting a broad range of effective alternatives in all aspects of supervision, curriculum development, and instruction. It will be equally helpful to teachers, administrators, supervisors, and the many other diverse audiences who are interested in the improvement of instruction.

PHIL C. ROBINSON
President, 1984-85
Association for Supervision and
Curriculum Development

Introduction

This work is the culmination of several years of research in developing and testing a differentiated system of supervision. Its essential thesis is that all teachers do not need clinical supervision and that experienced and competent teachers should have some options.

The work begins by establishing a rationale for such a differentiated approach, arguing from both the needs of the teacher and the resources of the organization. The next four chapters examine the four options to be offered to teachers: *clinical supervision*, the intensive observation and feedback conducted by a trained supervisor; *cooperative professional development*, in which small teams of peers work together for their mutual growth; *self-directed development*, in which the individual teacher assumes primary responsibility for his or her own growth; and *administrative monitoring*, a process by which the administrator conducts brief "drop-in" visits and conferences. Chapter 6 examines special resources that can be used in several of the optional modes: student feedback, videotape analysis, and the reflective journal. The last chapter suggests an implementation process that has been found to be generally effective. And I emphasize in the last chapter that each school should develop its own version of the system, after teachers, supervisors, and administrators have had an opportunity to discuss these ideas and examine their own needs.

Readers should understand that I do not offer the differentiated system as a definitive answer to the problem of providing effective supervision. Our experience in several field tests indicates that the system is feasible and suggests that it has positive effects on those who participate. But it is not a panacea for the ills of teaching. It will not be effective in all schools or with all teachers.

As noted above, the system has been developed through several years of pilot testing and research. I therefore wish to acknowledge my professional and personal indebtedness to all those doctoral students who implemented the pilot studies, conducted the evaluations, and helped me improve the differentiated approach through their constructive feedback: Joan Shapiro, Judy Beck, Julian Chalker, Earl Ball, Gary Cooper, and Sister Carmel Regina Shields. I also wish to thank all the supervisors, administrators, and teachers who cooperated in those studies.

Allan A. Glatthorn

1

A Rationale for Differentiated Supervision

Teachers should have some choice about the kind of supervision they receive—in contrast to the situation that prevails in most schools. In typical schools all teachers are observed once or twice a year by the principal, usually to evaluate performance. In some forward-looking schools the principal or supervisor tries to provide clinical supervision to all teachers. In neither situation are teachers given a choice. All are treated the same, even though they have very different needs.

In the differentiated system, teachers can choose, within limits, whether they wish to receive clinical supervision, work with a colleague in a program of cooperative development, direct their own professional growth, or have their teaching monitored by an administrator. They are given options, in the expectation that their individual choices will be more responsive to their special needs.

The Nature of Supervision

Before presenting a rationale for the differentiated approach, it might be useful to define more precisely the way the term *supervision* is used in this work. In many texts on supervision the term is used in its broadest sense. For example, Harris (1975) defines it this way:

> *What school personnel do with* adults *and* things *to maintain or change the school operation in ways that directly influence the teaching processes employed to promote pupil learning* (p. 10).

While such broad definitions are useful in examining the total supervisory function, they are too comprehensive for the present work, which is concerned primarily with the supervision of classroom instruction. In this work, therefore, the term is used with this meaning:

Supervision is a process of facilitating the professional growth of a teacher, primarily by giving the teacher feedback about classroom interactions and helping the teacher make use of that feedback in order to make teaching more effective.

This definition excludes some important methods of facilitating professional growth, such as providing inservice programs and involving the teacher in curriculum development. While such activities are clearly useful and productive, they are not the concern of this work. And the definition by its intent also excludes the *systematic* evaluation of teacher performance. Teacher evaluation is a critical function of school administration, but it should be perceived as a function distinct from supervision. If a school district decides to implement a differentiated supervision program, it is assumed that the district will continue to use whatever teacher evaluation system it has found effective.

So this monograph is concerned with a differentiated system of instructional supervision, one that gives the teacher some choice about how instruction is supervised.

A Rationale for the Differentiated System

Why is the system needed? There are three major reasons why a differentiated approach seems desirable.

First, the standard supervisory practice of administrators and supervisors is often both inadequate and ineffective. The findings of Lovell and Phelps (1976) about supervisory practices in Tennessee seem typical of the nation as a whole and, along with those of several other studies, provide evidence for the inadequacy of present practice. More than 80 percent of the teachers surveyed reported that they had not been observed during the year in question—and when observations were made, they typically were neither preceded nor followed by a conference. And other evidence about the ineffectiveness of standard supervisory practices is abundant. For example, 70 percent of the teachers in Young and Heichberger's (1975) survey indicated that they believe supervisors are often perceived as "potentially dangerous." And less than one-third of the teachers in Cawelti and Reavis's (1980) study rated their supervisory services as "high."

Second, it is neither feasible nor necessary to provide clinical supervision to all teachers. To begin with, clinical supervision is so time-consuming that it is not practical to use with all teachers. To understand this difficulty, consider the viewpoint of a supervisor in a large school system. During a 40-hour week, that supervisor probably spends about three hours a week on classroom observation and inservice education, if recent surveys can be trusted. (See Sullivan's 1982 survey for data on supervisory time allocations.) In a 36-week school year, therefore, that supervisor would be able to devote approximately 100 hours to instructional supervision—enough time to provide intensive clinical supervision to only 10 teachers, if the supervisor followed the guidelines offered by such experts as Goldhammer (1969) and Cogan (1973). Obviously, no district can afford to have one supervisor for every ten teachers.

Even if it were feasible to provide clinical supervision to all teachers, it would simply not be necessary. Clinical supervision was first developed to assist student teachers, and, according to Blumberg (1980) and other experts in the field of supervision, beginning teachers seem to profit most from its intensive scrutiny. There is no conclusive evidence that clinical supervision improves the performance of competent, experienced teachers. In fact, they often consider it the least useful of all the functions the supervisor can provide, as Ritz and Cashell's (1980) study noted. (See Chapter 2 for a more thorough review of the research on clinical supervision.)

The third argument in favor of differentiated supervision is that teachers have different growth needs and learning styles. They differ, first, in the type of interaction they prefer. Copeland's (1980) study is one of several that conclude that some teachers prefer a directive supervisory style, while others prefer non-directive interactions. Teachers differ also about the supervisory relationships they prefer. Young and Heichberger report that 62 percent of the teachers they surveyed preferred a "helping" relationship, while 36 percent wanted a "colleague-ship" relationship. And they differ in the kinds of environments in which they work and in their ability to learn in that environment. After studying several thousand teachers, Joyce and McKibbin (1982) concluded, "Enormous differences exist in the extent to which teachers pull growth-producing experiences from their environment and exploit personal and professional activities" (p. 36). And the irony, of course, is that administrators and supervisors who urge teachers to individualize their teaching rarely individualize their supervising.

How can supervision be individualized? One proposal that deserves careful attention is that advanced by Glickman (1981). After arguing that teachers can be classified as one of four types (analytical observers, teacher dropouts, professionals, and unfocused workers), Glickman recommends that the supervisor respond differentially to each type: "The supervisor can work toward that ideal [of enabling each teacher to become a Professional] by assessing the current levels of teacher development, taking each teacher at his or her level, and helping the teacher move toward the next stage of development" (p. 51). In a sense, Glickman's proposal offers the teacher four varieties of clinical supervision, depending on the teacher's present growth state.

While the Glickman proposal seems based on a sound rationale, it can be faulted on two grounds. First, I am reluctant to categorize teachers as he does. While I am aware of the research on adult learning styles, I do not believe that enough is known about adult growth to warrant attaching labels to complex individuals. Second, it seems unrealistic to hope that busy supervisors can find the time and marshal the energy to make individual assessments and respond uniquely to each teacher.

An Overview of the Differentiated System

The differentiated system advocated in this work takes a very different approach. Instead of categorizing teachers and responding to them accordingly, it lets teachers decide which options they wish. Instead of making more demands on supervisor time, it helps the supervisor focus his or her efforts where they are most critically needed. And instead of offering the teacher four varieties of clinical supervision, it gives the teacher a choice of four types of supervision: clinical supervision, cooperative professional development, self-directed development, and administrative monitoring.

Even though each option is explained more fully in the following four chapters, a brief overview should be useful at this point.

1. *Clinical supervision is an intensive process designed to improve instruction by conferring with a teacher on lesson planning, observing the lesson, analyzing the observational data, and giving the teacher feedback about the observation.* This clinical supervisory cycle is repeated several times throughout the year, as part of a systematic plan for professional growth developed by the supervisor and the teacher. Clinical

supervision should be provided by an administrator or supervisor trained in its special techniques. It seems to be most needed by beginning teachers, who are still acquiring the basic skills of teaching, and by experienced teachers who are encountering serious difficulties in the classroom.

2. *Cooperative professional development is a collegial process in which a small group of teachers agree to work together for their own professional growth.* They observe each other's classes, give each other feedback about those observations, and discuss common professional concerns. They can also collaborate in a range of other instructional activities, if they wish. It is much less intensive and systematic than clinical supervision, since the teachers are not trained in supervisory skills and do not have the time for long and involved conferences. It seems most useful for experienced, competent teachers who value collegiality.

3. *Self-directed development enables the individual teacher to work independently on professional growth concerns.* The teacher develops and carries out an individualized plan for professional growth, with the administrator or supervisor serving as a resource. Self-directed development seems most useful for experienced, competent teachers who prefer to work alone.

4. *Administrative monitoring, as the term implies, is a process by which an administrator monitors the work of the staff, making brief and unannounced visits simply to ensure that the staff are carrying out assignments and responsibilities in a professional manner.* While many texts on supervision scoff at such "drop-in" monitoring, there is persuasive evidence that such monitoring is a key aspect of the principal's role in instructional leadership. (See, for example, Leithwood and Montgomery's 1982 review.) All teachers can profit from such monitoring when it is performed by a sensitive and trusted leader. And it should be noted here that this monitoring, unlike the other three options, might include an evaluative element.

As is explained more fully in Chapter 7, there are many ways school systems can combine these options and make them available to teachers. In general, however, the research that my doctoral students and I have carried out indicates that the differentiated system works best when teachers are given a choice of the four options, with the principal maintaining the right to veto any choice considered unwise. (See Shields' 1982 study, for example.) And the choices usually made reflect the faculty diversity alluded to above. Thus, in a typical faculty of 50, the choices might be distributed in this fashion: clinical, 5; cooperative, 10; self-directed, 5; monitoring, 30.

Our research indicates that the differentiated system has several advantages. It responds to the individual needs of teachers by giving them a choice of supervisory mode. Obviously, it enables the administrator and supervisor to focus clinical efforts where they are most needed. (One principal can effectively provide clinical supervision to five teachers—but could not reasonably offer it to 50.) And our research indicates that implementing the system usually has a positive impact on teachers' perceptions of school climate. They value the fact that they are given a choice, and they appreciate the professional dialogue encouraged by the differentiated approach.

The differentiated system obviously is not without its own problems. The cooperative and self-directed options require teachers to invest some time and effort in their own professional development—and even some conscientious teachers are reluctant to give up any more time when they already are too busy and are feeling overworked. For maximum effectiveness, the differentiated system requires the active leadership of skilled and committed administrators and supervisors; such leaders are already busy coping with existing demands and are understandably hesitant to implement yet another time-consuming innovation. And as yet there is no solid evidence that the differentiated approach will result in improved teaching. The research on the total system and its several components for the most part has been of an exploratory sort; and while it has been encouraging, it is as yet not definitive.

But the differentiated approach can work. It's a feasible way to give teachers a choice and to enable supervisors to focus their energies where they are most needed. That seems reason enough to explore its components more fully and to examine how it can best be implemented.

2

Clinical Supervision

A s suggested in Chapter 1, one of the options that should be offered
teachers is clinical supervision. To make this component more
effective for those needing the clinical mode, this chapter attempts to
accomplish several related objectives: amplify the definition of clinical supervision; review the research on its effectiveness; describe current approaches to clinical supervision; explain in detail "learning-
centered supervision"; and discuss some implementation issues.

The Nature of Clinical Supervision

Clinical supervision, as defined in Chapter 1, is an intensive process
designed to improve instruction by conferring with the teacher on
lesson planning, observing the lesson, analyzing the observational
data, and giving the teacher feedback about the observation. This
definition, of course, presents a somewhat simplified picture of what is
a rather complex process. As Cogan (1973) sees clinical supervision, it
involves eight phases:

1. Establishing the supervisory relationship: build a relationship of
trust and support and induct the teacher into the role of co-supervisor.
2. Planning lessons and units with the teacher: determine objectives, concepts, teaching-learning techniques, materials, and assessment methods.

3. Planning the observation strategy: teacher and supervisor discuss the data to be gathered and the methods for gathering the data.

4. Observing in-class instruction.

5. Analyzing the observational data to determine patterns of behavior and critical incidents of teaching and learning.

6. Planning the conference strategy: set tentative conference objectives and processes.

7. Conferring to analyze data.

8. Resuming the planning: complete the cycle by determining future directions for growth and planning the next unit or lesson.

Other researchers, of course, have developed their own versions of the supervisory cycle in a clinical relationship, usually by reducing the number of and re-naming the phases. In general, however, most agree that the critical phases are planning, observing, analyzing, and providing feedback.

The Research on Clinical Supervision

What is known about the effectiveness of clinical supervision? After reviewing the available research on clinical supervision, Sullivan (1980) reaches a rather disheartening conclusion: ". . . the amount and quality of research is insufficient to support generalizations concerning the [clinical] model" (pp. 22–23). And in a rather recent work, Acheson and Gall (1980) note that they were not able to locate any studies proving that teachers who are clinically supervised produce better student achievement than teachers who are not so supervised. While it is unwise at this point to speak of "conclusions" and "reliable generalizations" about the effectiveness of clinical supervision, the research does suggest some tentative findings that can be used as guidelines by supervisors.

1. Teachers tend to favor a supervisor who is close and supportive (Gordon, 1976).

2. Most teachers and administrators agree with the basic assumptions of clinical supervision (Eaker, 1972).

3. Teachers seem to prefer clinical supervision to traditional supervision and believe that the techniques of clinical supervision are worthwhile (Reavis, 1977; Shinn, 1976).

4. Clinical supervision can change a teacher's behavior in the direction desired (Garman, 1971; Kerr, 1976; Krajewski, 1976; Shuma, 1973).

5. Supervisors using a clinical approach seem more open and accepting in post-observation conferences than those using a traditional approach (Reavis, 1977).

6. Teachers differ in the type of supervisory interactions they prefer; there is some evidence that experienced teachers prefer non-directive supervision, while beginning teachers seem to prefer a more direct style (Copeland, 1980).

These tentative findings, weak as they are, do not seem to provide a sufficient basis for relying on the standard components of clinical supervision as the only system for improving instruction. Consequently, there has been a great deal of interest among supervision leaders in developing improved versions of or alternatives to the standard approach to clinical supervision.

Current Approaches to Clinical Supervision

Three major alternatives seem worthy of serious consideration: scientific supervision, accountable supervision, and artistic supervision.

Scientific Supervision

Scientific supervision is clinical supervision that focuses on those teacher behaviors that its advocates claim are clearly supported by scientific research. (For an excellent review of the history and claims of scientific supervision, see McNeil, 1982). Perhaps the most well known of the scientific approaches is that of Madeline Hunter, who, after reviewing the research on teaching and learning, prescribes a model of teaching with nine specific components (Russell and Hunter, 1980).

1. *Diagnosis.* Identify a general objective and assess pupils' present attainment in relation to it.

2. *Specific objectives.* On the basis of the diagnosis, select a specific objective for the daily lesson.

3. *Anticipatory set.* Focus attention, review previous learning, and develop readiness for what is to come.

4. *Perceived purpose.* Clarify the objective for the pupils, explain its importance, and relate it to previous learning.

5. *Learning opportunities.* Choose learning opportunities that will help learners achieve objectives.

6. *Modeling.* Provide both a verbal and a visual example of what is to be learned.

7. *Check for understanding.* Assess the extent to which pupils are achieving objectives.

8. *Guided practice.* Guide pupils' practice of learning, checking to see that they can perform successfully.

9. *Independent practice.* Give pupils opportunity to practice the new skill on their own.

The Hunter model and others similar to it seem to be gaining wide acceptance in the profession for what are perhaps obvious reasons. First, they appeal because they are *teacher-centered.* While they vary in their particulars, in essence they all seem to be essentially similar versions of direct instruction: a set of teacher-centered pedagogical techniques that have generally appealed to most teachers. They also appeal because they appear to be *research-based.* The scientific models, their advocates claim, are supported by several studies of teacher effectiveness, which indicate that in general pupil achievement (as measured by standardized achievement tests) improves when teachers use the methods espoused. (See, for example, Medley's 1979 review.) And the scientific models appeal because of their *simplicity;* they say, in essence, "Here's a nine-step prescription for successful teaching."

The scientific models, of course, are not without their critics. Fenstermacher (1978) observes that the direct instruction research supporting the scientific models does not give sufficient attention to the intentions of the teacher. Peterson (1979) notes that the research supporting direct instruction is not persuasive. Her review of all the studies supposedly favoring direct instruction points out that only small effects are attributable to direct instruction. She further notes that the research tends to show that "open classroom" techniques, when compared to direct instruction methods, lead to greater creativity and more positive attitudes toward learning. Calfee (1981) is even more critical of its narrowness:

> The investigations [from which the direct instruction model derives] have tended to be empirical, behavioral, correlational, and prescriptive: the typical study lacks theoretical foundation, focuses on action more than thought, entails interventions that are poorly controlled, yet eventuates in advice to the teacher on how to conduct classroom instruction... (p. 53).

However, the greatest weakness of the Hunter model and those similar to it is that they present one model of teaching as if it were the only model. Observe the difficulty in trying to apply the Hunter nine-step prescription to an inquiry lesson in science or a creative project in industrial arts. It makes more sense to see teaching as diverse and various, as Joyce and Weil (1980) see it. Those familiar with their work will remember that they describe 23 models of teaching, not just one.

Accountable Supervision

Accountable supervision is concerned not with what the teacher does but with what the pupil learns. As described by McNeil (1971), the supervisor who uses an "accountable" approach begins by helping the teacher determine what learning objectives will be emphasized during a given lesson. The supervisor and teacher also agree in the planning conference about how learning will be assessed. Then, when the supervisor visits the classroom, he or she observes primarily to determine whether pupils have achieved the intended objective. Issues of teaching method are considered only in light of pupil attainment: if a particular method seems to help that group of pupils learn with that teacher, then it is considered praiseworthy—as long as there are no undesirable side-effects, such as boredom or negative attitudes toward the subject matter.

There is some evidence to support the usefulness of this approach. Young and Heichberger (1975) indicated that 70 percent of the teachers they surveyed approved of the supervisor and teacher agreeing on instructional objectives and then working together to evaluate those objectives. And a study by Smithman and Lucio (1974) concluded that pupils whose teachers were evaluated by objectives outperformed those whose teachers were evaluated on a rating scale. Those who are reluctant to embrace the model typically express the reservations that the term *accountable* usually elicits: measurable objectives are often the least important outcomes of teaching; an emphasis on measurement causes teachers to set only narrow and easily attained goals; and the assessment measures ordinarily used by teachers in the classroom do not validly measure affective and higher-order cognitive goals.

Artistic Supervision

Artistic supervision is an approach to supervision developed chiefly by Elliot Eisner (1982), who defines it as:

> . . . *an approach to supervision that relies on the sensitivity, perceptivity, and knowledge of the supervisor as a way of appreciating the significant subtleties occurring in the classroom, and that exploits the expressive, poetic, and often metaphorical potential of language*

to convey to teachers or to others whose decisions affect what goes on in schools, what has been observed (p. 59).

Eisner sees the supervisor as a connoisseur of teaching who attempts to appreciate both the overall quality and the distinctive character of the performance. The supervisor then reports those perceptions in the language of educational criticism, which Eisner sees as analogous to film criticism and music criticism—language that helps others appreciate what has been created or performed.

While as yet there appear to be no reports of its effectiveness, the accounts of artistic supervision reported in Eisner's works (see, for example, *The Educational Imagination*, 1979) seem to provide evidence of the usefulness of this approach. Those trained in artistic supervision can obviously render accounts of teaching that complement the standard "objective" reports of the clinical supervisor. These accounts, written by Eisner's students, are impressionistic, rather than attempting to be objective; they strive to capture the whole world of the classroom, rather than focusing solely on the teacher's behavior; and their language is metaphoric and replete with sensory images, rather than being entirely literal. And, perhaps most important, they attempt to interpret the meaning of the classroom world, rather than evaluating or changing the behavior of the participants in that world.

Rather than being perceived as a substitute for other forms of supervision, artistic supervision is perhaps more wisely used as a complement to the scientific and accountable approaches. As Sergiovanni (1982) notes, its chief value is in providing a theoretical-normative avenue to knowledge: it interprets the meaning of the classroom by examining the teacher's belief system as it determines classroom life.

Learning-Centered Supervision

Each of these three approaches to supervision has advantages and disadvantages. In the process of training supervisors and directing doctoral research on supervision, I have developed an approach—which I call *learning-centered supervision*—that attempts to build upon the strengths of these three, while adding its own particular emphases. Learning-centered supervision is concerned with helping teachers learn about their own teaching and its effects, so that they can become active problem solvers in their own classrooms; it posits the learning activities of students as the appropriate focus of the classroom observation; and it attempts to facilitate the learning of the supervisor by using the teacher as a source of feedback. It includes seven major components: opening conference, pre-observation conference, unfocused observation, focused observation, observational analysis, feedback conference, and formative assessment conference.

Opening Conference

This initial conference is more than just a friendly "get-acquainted" session. It is a time to accomplish three important purposes: identify any immediate problems that need attention; share views about professional issues; and develop the supervisory contract. As Figure 1 indicates, you begin the conference by helping the teacher feel at ease and by laying out the purposes of the conference. You then turn your attention to any specific problems that the teacher needs help with: textbooks not available, supplies not provided, schedule unclear, and so on. These concerns are a good place to begin because they are probably foremost in the teacher's mind. It is difficult to think clearly about long-term problems until today's vexations are dealt with. By beginning with these practical concerns, you also convey the impression that your function is to help, not to evaluate.

Figure 1. Opening Conference Agenda

1. Establish a comfortable atmosphere and explain conference purpose.
2. Discover if any immediate problems require attention.
3. Explore teacher's and share supervisor's views about:
   a. The nature of the learner.
   b. The purposes of schooling.
   c. The school curriculum and the subject taught.
   d. Approach to teaching and general teaching style.
   e. Preferences about lesson planning.
   f. Classroom environment and classroom management.
   g. The supervisory relationship: supervision as mutual learning.
4. Discuss the supervisory contract:
   a. Who will observe?
   b. How often will observations be made?
   c. Will they be announced or unannounced—or both?
   d. Will observational data from supervisory visits be shared with evaluators?
   e. Will a pre-observation conference always be held?
   f. What form will feedback take—and when will it occur?
   g. What does the supervisor expect about the courtesies of the visit—should lesson plans be offered, textbook made available, presence acknowledged, participation invited?
   h. May the teacher request that an unannounced visit be deferred?
   i. What other supervisory resources are available to the teacher?
5. Close conference on positive note.

It is wise to limit this phase of the conference: answer questions, make clear what you cannot do, and make notes on items requiring a follow-up. My experience suggests that ten minutes should be ample. Then move the conference to the next phase: sharing views.

I emphasize the *sharing* aspect of this next phase. It is a time for you to understand the teacher's beliefs; but it is also a time to make clear your own theories and principles. This exchange shows how the sharing might take place:

Supervisor: I'd be interested in hearing you talk about the kind of classroom environment you would like to have. (*Asks open question.*)

Teacher: Middle school youngsters need a firm hand. I think I take a no-nonsense approach to classroom discipline.

Supervisor: You see yourself as very task-oriented then? (*Reflects to invite fuller explanation.*)

Teacher: I think so. I have work on the board when they walk into the room. I push hard. I keep them busy. I try to keep them working right up to the bell. That way there's never any trouble.

Supervisor: In general the research supports your approach, at least when it comes to pupil achievement. But my experience suggests that middle school youngsters will have better attitudes about a classroom where there is some informality, an occasional break from task-engagement. (*Affirms general tenor of comment; begins to explore area of difference.*) How do you feel about that matter? (*Invites response and discussion.*)

Notice that the supervisor takes time to listen to and understand the teacher's approach to classroom environment. Her question of reflection gives him a chance to make clear that he is highly task-oriented in working with middle school learners. The supervisor then begins to explore an area of difference; she doesn't simply accept his position with a non-directive response. She wants to be sure that her own values here are made explicit. Yet she does so without being heavy-handed; her question invites further discussion.

This open exchange of views might touch on all the issues identified in Figure 1—or it might focus on only a few. Regardless of the number of issues discussed, there are two central objectives of this phase of the opening conference: (1) to establish a climate of mutual openness, and (2) to stress that the goal is mutual learning.

With that orientation established, the next step is the supervisory contract. That discussion of the contract will, of course, have to be more directive in its tone, since for the most part you will be explaining district policies, not negotiating an agreement. Figure 1 lists the specific items that probably need to be covered. It might be useful to prepare a question-answer sheet dealing with these issues, since it is important for both parties to have a clear understanding about these matters. Such a sheet might be presented in this way:

> *If I may, I'd like to move now to a discussion of the specifics of our supervisory relationship. I've prepared a handout that lists most of the questions our teachers have about supervision, along with the answers we've come up with so far. I'd like you to take a copy of this along with you, and perhaps we could talk for a few minutes now about some of the more important items.*

The opening conference closes with the supervisor making a few summary observations and noting that he or she anticipates a productive supervisory relationship with the teacher.

Pre-Observation Conference

Experts in clinical supervision seem to agree that every observation should be preceded by a pre-observation conference. However, there are occasions when you may see fit to deviate from this practice. You and the teacher might agree that you have such a clear understanding of the teacher's planning and teaching methods that some pre-observation conferences might be well omitted. You may feel so pressed for time that you decide to omit a pre-observation conference during one particular cycle. Or you may find that you have some time available for observation on a day when you had not planned to observe—and you visit unannounced, without having held a pre-observation conference. In general, however, the pre-observation conference is so useful that it should be a basic part of the supervisory cycle.

It might be appropriate at this point to discuss the issue of announced and unannounced visits. For the most part supervisory visits should be announced and planned. Announcing or agreeing about the date and time of a forthcoming visit gives you and the teacher an opportunity to discuss in detail the teacher's plans for that class. And, as noted more fully below, this discussion of planning can be one of the most effective aspects of the supervisory process. On the other hand, an announced visit will make some teachers unduly anxious and apprehensive; they prefer unannounced visits. And announcing a visit makes it more likely that you will see an atypical performance: the teacher might make special plans or coach the students.

One solution to this dilemma is to inform the teacher about the general plan to visit, without providing details about day and period:

I'd like to visit one of your 7th-grade classes some time this week. Is there any date that would not be good for you? Could you give me a general idea of what your 7th-graders are studying, so that I can be better prepared?

The agenda suggested in Figure 2 is appropriate for an announced visit. You begin by asking the teacher to give you a general sense of the class—their ability, their characteristics as a group—and to inform you of any students who have special problems. You then ask the teacher to talk about their general academic progress. What unit is being studied? How does that unit relate to the instructional goals of that year?

Figure 2. Pre-Observation Conference Agenda

1. What are the general characteristics of this class? What should an observer know about them as a group?
2. Are any individual students experiencing learning or behavior problems?
3. What general academic progress have they made? Where are they in relation to your goals for the year?
4. What are your specific objectives for the class session to be observed?
5. What is your general pacing strategy? About how much time do you plan to devote to each major objective?
6. What teaching methods and learning activities do you plan to use in order to accomplish those objectives?
7. How do you plan to assess learning and give students feedback?
8. What alternative scenarios have you thought about in case one of the planned activities does not work out?
9. Is this observation to be unfocused or focused? If focused, what will be the focus of the observation?

With this general background presented, you then move the discussion to four important aspects of planning: objectives, pace of learning, methods, and assessment strategies. Each will require careful analysis and discussion. In such an analysis, should you be somewhat non-directive or more directive in your approach? The answer is not a simple one. Consider these factors:

• Teachers vary in their preferences. Some teachers prefer supervisors who are more directive.
• Teachers vary in their needs. Some beginning teachers do not have enough experience to respond profitably to a non-directive conference.

- Supervisors have their own preferred ways of interacting with other professionals.
- The research is not conclusive in supporting one style over another.

As you think through this issue, keep in mind the dangers of giving too much advice. If you become too directive and tell the teacher what to do, then the teacher takes *your* plan to the classroom. If things go badly, the response from the teacher is predictable: "Your ideas didn't work out so well."

For the most part, learning-centered supervision calls for a *problem-solving* style: you participate actively in the conference, helping the teacher solve the planning problems. You pose questions, help the teacher anticipate consequences, assist the teacher in thinking about options, offer data. You avoid the passive, non-directive style of simply acknowledging and reflecting; and you avoid the leading, directive style of giving advice and making judgments. Here's an example of the problem-solving style at work in a pre-observation conference:

Supervisor: How do you plan to help your students think about the audience for whom they are writing? (*Raises question about method.*)

Teacher: I thought I would have them do some role playing. They'll be writing a speech addressed to adults, so I thought I'd put them in small groups, with the other group members playing the role of somewhat hostile adults.

Supervisor: Sounds like an interesting activity. Have they had any experience this year in role playing? (*Affirms one value of method — helps teacher think about student readiness.*)

Teacher: No, this is the first time for us. They might have done it last year with another teacher.

Supervisor: Maybe. But in a sense, every year is a fresh beginning for students. If they haven't done it before—or if they have forgotten, what problems might you anticipate? (*Offers data; asks teacher to think about possible problems.*)

Teacher: Well, I'm worried that they might turn it into a big joke— you know, a lot of giggling and fooling around.

Supervisor: I think you're right. Let's think together about what you might do to prevent that from happening. (*Sets stage for problem solving.*)

Such a style makes the teacher an active participant in solving planning problems and results in an instructional plan for which he or she feels responsible.

The eighth item on the conference agenda (see Figure 2) asks the teacher to think about alternative scenarios. Even the best plans go awry: films do not arrive on time; equipment does not operate; students do not respond to the activity as hoped; or they arrive in class without having done the assigned work. A good teacher always has alternative plans in mind; and a good supervisor helps the teacher develop such "what-if" alternatives. And the last agenda item, of course, relates to the nature of the forthcoming conference. As explained more fully below, learning-centered supervision alternates *unfocused* observations (the supervisor attempts to observe and note all relevant behavior), with *focused* observations (the supervisor observes and notes only one type of behavior). If the next observation is to be focused, teacher and supervisor both agree about its specific focus.

One reason this pre-observation conference is so important is that teachers seem more open and feel less threatened when they talk about what they might do *in the future*. They do not have as much ego invested in plans as they do in performances. Once they have taught in a particular way, they feel inclined to defend their actions, even when such actions have produced undesirable results.

The Relationship Between Unfocused and Focused Observations

Let's consider these two methods in relationship with each other, before discussing them separately, since that relationship is an important component of learning-centered supervision. The overall strategy goes like this:

1. Begin with an unfocused observation in which you attempt to observe and note all significant behavior; observe like a camera that holds the entire scene in view.

2. Analyze the observational data to determine situations in which learning seems to be facilitated and when it seems to be impeded. To plan for the feedback conference, tentatively identify some problems that may need attention and some strengths that the teacher can build upon.

3. Hold a problem-solving feedback conference, in which you use the observational data to help the teacher identify an important problem and make plans to solve that problem. As an outcome of the feedback conference, determine with the teacher what specific aspect of learning and teaching will be the focus of the next observation.

4. Hold the focused observation as planned, gathering only those data that relate to the problem identified.

5. Analyze the data from the focused observation to plan for another problem-solving conference.

6. Hold another problem-solving conference; as a result of the problem solving, determine if the next observation will be unfocused or focused.

This alternation between unfocused and focused observation is neither inflexible nor capricious. Instead, it results from collaborative problem solving between teacher and supervisor, as they decide what type of observation (and what focus, if any) will help the teacher continue to develop professionally. Thus, the supervisor and the teacher are partners in a shared inquiry, examining together three related questions: *What is going on in this classroom? What changes might be made to improve learning? What type of observation seems most useful at this point?*

With this general strategy established and its rationale explicated, let's examine both types of observation in greater detail.

Unfocused Observation

Each supervisor will have a distinct way of making an unfocused observation. Below is a sketch of one method that seems to be effective.

If possible, plan to arrive at a beginning point—the start of a period in secondary school or the beginning of the morning or afternoon session in elementary school. Arriving at one of these transition points will generate useful information about how the teacher handles this crucial phase of the class meeting—how the teacher gets the class settled, handles the necessary administrative business, and begins the first learning episode. You then begin to observe.

What do you observe for—and what kinds of notes do you take? The usual advice is to take verbatim notes of all that occurs. If you want to use a moderately structured form to facilitate making a chronological record of all that occurs, you might find a form like the one shown in Figure 3 to be useful. Note the time. You identify the teacher's objective, either recording what the teacher explicitly says about the objective or inferring from the teacher's actions what was probably intended. Then note the actions the teacher took to achieve those objectives and the responses the students made to those actions. This form yields a running account of the three essential components of the learning transaction: *teacher objectives, teacher actions, student responses.*

Figure 3. Teacher-Centered Observation Form

Teacher: *Lisa Lopatin*   **Date:** *10/28/83*   **Time:** *11:00 a.m.*

Time	Teacher Objectives	Teacher Actions	Student Responses
11:00	*Stimulate interest in writing*	*Discusses Halloween with children: what they are going to be*	*Call out ideas*
11:02	*Get children to discuss ideas in more orderly fashion*	*Reminds children to raise hands and wait turn*	*Call out ideas*
11:04	*Provide children with working vocabulary*	*Writes ideas on board*	*Call out ideas*
11:08	*Have children write*	*Passes out paper*	*Call out questions*
11:10	*Have children write a complete sentence*	*Writes on board: I want to be _____*	*Call out questions*
11:14	*Facilitate children's writing*	*Walks around room, spelling words*	*Call out questions/ for clarification of task*
11:19	*Facilitate children's writing*	*Walks around room, spelling words*	*Six out of 22 children on-task*
11:22	*Facilitate children's writing*	*Walks around room, spelling words*	*Six out of 22 children on-task*
11:25	*Facilitate children's writing*	*Explains children should find something quiet to do when finished*	*Four children on-task*
11:28	*Conclude lesson*	*Asks children to hand in papers*	*Children pass papers, talking loudly, out of seats*

Some experts who advocate scientific supervision suggest using the Madeline Hunter prescription (or some variety thereof) as the basis of an observational form. For example, Minton (1982) suggests using a form that will enable the supervisor to answer the following questions. Did the teacher:

- Set reasonably high standards for the pupils?
- Develop anticipatory set, clarifying the objective, relating new learning to previous learning, and motivating learning?
- Assess prior learning?
- Provide input, model, and check for understanding?
- Provide guided practice for the learning?
- Help pupils achieve closure?
- Provide opportunities for independent practice?

Such observational methods that focus on the critical acts of teaching are useful, of course. Since they provide the observer and the teacher with a clear set of guidelines, there is no uncertainty about the foci of the observation. And they help the observer especially to focus on what seem to be the important teaching functions, reducing the likelihood that the observation report will be filled with general or irrelevant comments. They also readily establish a basis for the shared discussion of teaching: supervisor and teacher use a common vocabulary.

There are, however, two serious limitations in using such forms to observe all teachers in all subject fields. Both limitations stem from the fact that these forms are all based on a single model of teaching—direct instruction that is primarily verbal in nature. First, they focus unduly on the teacher, shifting the observer's attention away from the pupils and their interactions and responses. Second, they unnecessarily and unwisely restrict the range of desirable teaching-learning behaviors to those that will fit the direct instruction model. To understand this second limitation, ask yourself how useful such forms would be for observing the following kinds of learning:

- An art class—students are working on their own creative projects.
- An English class—students in small groups are doing a guided fantasy as a pre-writing activity, with very little direction from the teacher.
- A social studies class—students are using primary sources to reach their own conclusions about the impact of the early Suffragettes.
- A home economics class—students are working independently to develop plans for decorating their own bedrooms.

Direct instruction forms just do not seem to work well in observing teaching and learning that emphasize creativity, discovery, non-verbal learning, group processes, and independent inquiry. They appear to work well in teacher-directed, traditional classrooms; they would probably not work well in laboratories, open classrooms, and learning centers.

Learning-centered supervision, instead of focusing initially on teacher behaviors, begins by looking at the learning activities of the pupils and then examines teacher behaviors as they seem to be facilitating or impeding learning. It asks: What are the pupils doing in this classroom? Are their activities learning-oriented? What has the teacher done to bring about this condition? To facilitate such observation, the form shown in Figure 4 was developed and field-tested in a wide range of classrooms. Developed from a review of the theory and research on school learning, the form is structured around the three basic phases of learning—*readiness, engagement,* and *closure*—and identifies 16 specific behaviors that might be observed when pupils are learning. It then provides space for the observer to note relevant teacher behaviors—those that seem to be impeding or facilitating learning.

Note that the form is designed so that the observer can closely examine a particular learning episode—a related series of learning activities designed to achieve a major learning objective. In a typical class period or instructional session, you might expect to find from two to four such episodes. As an observer you could decide to observe only one episode, using a single form, or to observe all, using one form for each episode.

Obviously, the form can be used in traditional classrooms. But its main value is that it can be used effectively in other kinds of learning environments, since its focus is on learning, not teaching. Suppose you have entered an art classroom. You observe that the teacher is working with one student. All other students seem busily engaged. You confer briefly with six students. Four of them seem to have high expectations and standards for their work. Two do not; they seem to be satisfied with simply getting the job done. You note those observations on the form. At that moment you cannot observe what the teacher has or has not done to help the students set high standards. You make a note to talk with the teacher about the issue of standards and expectations—to explore in a problem-solving conference the discrepancy between student-set standards and teacher expectations. You do not begin by assuming that setting standards is solely the teacher's responsibility.

Figure 4. Learner-Centered Observation Form

Stage	Desirable Learning Behaviors	Facilitating Teacher Behaviors	Impeding Teacher Behaviors
R E A D I N E S S	1. Learns important skills, concepts, at appropriate level of difficulty 2. Believes in ability to learn, sets high standards 3. Perceives learning as relevant 4. Has prior skill and knowledge required for learning task 5. Understands learning objectives	*Models content of lesson with appealing poem* *Commends previous writing and states looking forward to results of present effort*	
E N G A G E M E N T	6. Gets overview of learning and its connections 7. Actively engages in task-related activities 8. Uses varied, challenging materials 9. Remains on-task 10. Paces learning appropriately 11. Gets feedback about performance 12. Practices, applies learning in related situations 13. With effort achieves mastery of objectives at satisfactory level 14. Takes corrective measures when standard has not been met	*Provides students choice and materials adaptable to level of ability* *Interested, encouraging; comments on student work*	*Didn't attend to child not on-task*
C L O S U R E	15. Synthesizes and integrates learning, approaches closure 16. Anticipates and prepares for next learning task	*Shares student writing and encourages awareness*	

Additional Observations:

You do not fault the teacher when you note that some students have set easily attained goals. You observe learners in an environment, you make notes about their learning, and you raise questions about the role of the teacher. You make an unfocused learning-centered observation.

Focused Observation

After you have completed one or more unfocused observations, you and the teacher will probably agree that a focused observation would be helpful. What can such observations focus on? The answer, obviously, should be determined by both parties. You might decide to focus on one of the nine aspects listed in Figure 5, which the research suggests affect pupil achievement.

Figure 5. Suggested Foci for Classroom Observation

1. How efficient is the teacher's use of time? How much time is spent in classroom business, in disciplining, in learning, in personal business?
2. How effective is the teacher as an explainer of concepts? Does the teacher present an overview, relate the new concept to ones previously learned, provide clear definitions, give many examples?
3. How effective are the teacher's questioning skills? Does the teacher have a planned sequence in mind? Does the teacher ask both memory and thinking questions, as well as creative and personal questions?
4. How effective are the teacher's responding skills? Does the teacher use student answers? Does the teacher give negative and positive feedback as appropriate?
5. How appropriate and clear are the learning objectives? Is the level of difficulty appropriate to these learners? Are the objectives made clear? Does the teacher make the objectives relevant to pupils?
6. How appropriate and effective are the learning activities? Are there a sufficient number of active learning strategies? Do activities seem appropriate to the objectives? Is the relationship between objectives and activities made clear to the pupils?
7. How effective are the teacher's assessment strategies? Does the teacher make frequent assessment of pupil learning? Is the learning of all pupils assessed adequately? Do pupils get feedback about performance?
8. How appropriate are the teacher's interactions with pupils? Who volunteers? Who is called on? How does the teacher respond to incorrect answers? To whom does the teacher talk before and after class? How would the classroom climate be characterized?
9. How effective are the teacher's classroom management behaviors? Is the teacher clear about the kind of learning environment desired? Does the teacher make clear those expectations? Does the teacher keep pupils on-task without interfering with learning? Does the teacher deal with off-task behavior appropriately? Is the teacher aware of all that is going on in the classroom?

Another approach is to focus even more sharply on one particular type of learning. For example, Figure 6 shows a form I developed to assist a supervisor in observing an English language arts teacher conducting pre-writing activities in a composition unit. Here the form is structured around the nature of the teaching-learning task, not a particular teaching technique.

Once you have determined the particular focus of the observation, you then should develop a form that will help in gathering the observational data. As noted above, one special benefit of the focused observation is that it can yield very specific data that will enable you and the teacher to identify significant strengths and weaknesses; you therefore need a form that will yield very specific information, not general impressions.

Use this process in designing the focused observation form:

1. Identify the focus of the observation.
2. Review the literature relating to that behavior to help identify its salient aspects.
3. Consider the general nature of the form you want. If you want information about what happens over time, then the form should be time-structured. If you want information about how the teacher relates to particular students, then the form should list students' names.
4. Develop a rough draft of the form. Ask a few experienced teachers to review it and give you input about improving it.
5. Try out the revised form in an actual observation. Make further refinements.
6. Share it with your colleagues when it seems easy to use and gives useful data.

Figure 7 shows a form I developed to obtain focused data on a teacher's explaining skills. After reviewing the literature on lecturing, explaining, and concept formation, I identified the behaviors listed. I then decided that the supervisor would probably want specific information about how effectively the teacher used those skills with each concept, principle, or class of information presented. Next, I worked out a simple code that would enable an untrained observer to make the observations needed. Supervisors who want additional information about the development and use of focused observation forms should consult Good and Brophy (1978) for an excellent source book on classroom observation.

Figure 6. Learning-Specific Observation Form: Pre-Writing Activities

Teacher: *Carol Bliven*   **Date:** *11/4/83*   **Time:** *9:00 a.m.*   **Supervisor:** *Betty Parpart*

Pre-Writing Objectives	Was the teacher concerned with the objective?	What methods were used to achieve the objective?	Student responses suggesting success	Student responses suggesting problems
1. Stimulate interest in writing	*Yes*	*Role play*	*Five students on-task, eager to write*	*Six students seemed confused, asked questions*
2. Help students explore topic, audience, purpose				
3. Help students retrieve, systematize information				
4. Help students develop needed thinking skills				
5. Help students plan writing				

Figure 7. Focused Observation Form: Explaining Skills

Teacher: *Mildred Irene* **Date:** *2/23/83* **Period:** *3* **Supervisor:** *Leonard Mason*

Main topic of lesson: *Causes of Civil War*

Concept	Gave overview	Made con- nections	Explained clearly	Gave clear examples	Used visuals	Made transitions
1. Nature of cause	o	xx	x	x	o	o
2. Economic causes	o	x	x	x	o	o
3. Political causes	o	xx	x	x	o	o
4. Ideological causes	o	x	o	o	o	o

Code: **o:** **Teacher did not seem to make use of this skill.**
 x: **Teacher made satisfactory use of this skill.**
 xx: **Teacher made more than satisfactory use of this skill.**

Observational Analysis

You have made an unfocused or a focused observation, and you have taken detailed notes about what you observed. Now you prepare for the feedback conference by making a careful analysis of your notes and your subjective impressions of the class. These are the central questions you want to answer in your analysis: *To what extent was learning taking place in that classroom? In what ways was the teacher's behavior facilitating or impeding that learning?*

You should not be concerned with rating the teacher, or with personal factors such as the teacher's dress, voice, or behavioral idiosyncrasies. Neither should your worry about how the teacher's approach differed from one you might have used. Your focus should be on learning—and the ways in which the teaching facilitated or impeded that learning.

If you have done a *focused* observation, the analysis is a relatively simple matter. You review the focused data, noting the significant information that seems worth discussing in the feedback conference. As explained more fully below, the feedback conference following a focused observation may consist of the observer simply handing the focused observation form to the teacher so that the two of them can examine it together. This simple sharing of the form means that the preceding analysis need concern itself only with major problems and strengths. Review, for example, the "explaining skills" form shown in Figure 7. As the supervisor, you obviously would want to praise the teacher for consistently relating the new concept to what the students already know. The weaknesses would be similarly apparent: no overview, no use of graphics or visuals, and no clear transitions to the next concept.

The analysis of *unfocused* observational data is much more difficult. You probably have more data to deal with, and the data relate to several aspects of the teaching-learning transaction. The difficulty of the analysis will, of course, be affected by the kinds of notes you have taken and the form you have used. Use of the less structured observation form shown in Figure 3 will require a very careful examination of each series of transactions, noting those that yielded a positive student response and those that seemingly caused problems. If you have used the learning-centered form shown in Figure 4, then the analysis is somewhat simplified. The form shows you at a glance which behaviors were facilitating and which were impeding—and relates those to stages in the learning process.

Regardless of the kind of notes taken or form used, you should probably make a simple chart. In the left-hand column, list all the teacher behaviors that seemed to be having a positive or facilitating effect, with a brief note reminding you when those behaviors occurred or citing a particular example of that behavior. Make a list of the negative or impeding behaviors in the right-hand column. Then prioritize each item in the two lists, perhaps using a code like this one:

1 = A very important behavior; probably should be discussed in this conference.

2 = A somewhat important behavior; might be discussed in this conference.

3 = A less important behavior; probably should not be discussed in this conference.

Several matters should be considered when weighing the importance of the items. First, you should consider the importance of the behavior as it relates to teaching and learning. Some behaviors, like closely monitoring student attention, have a major impact on achievement. Other behaviors, like re-directing pupil responses, seem to have less of an impact. You should also weigh the importance of the behavior to that particular teacher. Where is that teacher in his or her professional development? What skills is he or she ready to learn? Some teaching skills, like using metaphors to teach creative thinking, are so complex that only very experienced teachers seem ready to master them. Finally, you should assess the importance of that behavior in terms of the frequency of its occurrence. If a teacher makes an impeding move several times during the lesson, the frequency suggests that the behavior is more typical and perhaps more deeply ingrained.

A general rule of thumb in prioritizing is to limit the # 1 rating (very important) to no more than two facilitating and two impeding behaviors. As will be explained more fully below, the feedback conference should emphasize a smaller number of facilitating and impeding actions, rather than trying to cover a long agenda of teaching problems. Figure 8 shows how such a listing and prioritizing might be done.

Should you prepare a formal observation report following your classroom visit? The answer depends, of course, on district policy and your own preferences. Four options are possible.

1. Do not write a formal report. Simply note in your own records when you observed and conferred, relying chiefly on the face-to-face conference as the feedback medium. This option is desirable unless your district requires written reports of all supervisory visits.

Figure 8. Supervisor's Form for Analysis and Prioritizing

Teacher: *Alex Clemson*   **Date:** *4/16/83*   **Period:** *3*   **Supervisor:** *Stanley Moon*

Facilitating Behaviors	Priority	Impeding Behaviors	Priority
Knew students' names	*2*	*Not much active learning (listen-recite, except for one student at board)*	*1*
Related learning to lives (many references to Hispanic terms)	*1*	*Most questions were factual (who, when, define)*	*3*
Monitored learning closely (quiz at start, much oral questioning)	*1*	*Selective calling on students (all in middle of room)*	*2*
Used nonverbal supportive responses (smiles, nods)	*2*	*Too much reliance on verbal learning (no use of visuals)*	*1*
		Slow getting class started (five minutes taking roll, signing notes)	*2*
		Seemed unaware of two inattentive students	*3*

2. Submit your observation form as the report. This choice is probably not a wise one, since the observation notes are raw data intended to help you confer with the teacher.

3. Prepare a brief report for the record, providing space for the teacher to add comments. If you prepare such a report, it seems most useful to give it to the teacher at the end of the feedback conference, noting that it can be amended. Figure 9 shows one form that has been used for this purpose. Notice that it begins with an account of the major transactions of the lesson, includes both facilitating and impeding teacher behaviors, and provides room for teacher comments.

4. Prepare a fully detailed written report. You rely on this as the primary method of feedback, using the conference chiefly for a brief discussion of key issues. This option seems least desirable. The supervisory process is an interactive process that requires open discussion of learning and teaching concerns—and the written report impedes such open discussion.

Figure 9. Supervisory Report Form

Teacher: *Deborah Epstein*   **Date:** *10/11/83*   **Time:** *1:00 p.m.*
Supervisor: *Carol Kramer*

Narrative record of important teaching-learning transactions:

1. *Teacher assembles children on rug at front of room (having selected two boys to clear the area of chairs left from previous activity). Children move quickly and smoothly from their desks to the rug.*
2. *Teacher questions children to review rhyming patterns and extending phrases in poetry as concretized in the poem "The House That Jack Built" used in the previous writing lesson. Students readily answer the teacher's questions.*
3. *Teacher introduces a new poem to children: "The Jam That Pam Made," explaining that it is very much like "The House That Jack Built" in that it contains rhyme and extending phrases.*
4. *Teacher distributes copy of new poem to children, reads the poem, and invites children to read the poem with her.*
5. *Teacher discusses the poem with children, asking questions about rhyming words, vocabulary, and the sequence of events.*
6. *Children ask to read the poem again. Teacher selects students to read a line at a time, then invites all students to read the poem together once again.*
7. *Teacher distributes a worksheet to the children and explains that their task is to: (1) notice that the sheet contains ten boxes–each containing one word; (2) cut the words apart along the dotted lines enclosing each word; (3) arrange the words on their desks into as many sentences as they can; (4) write the sentences on paper, if they wish.*
8. *Teacher asks if all children understand the assigned task. She sends those children who indicate they understand to their desks to begin. She keeps five children with her who indicated they did not understand. The teacher re-explains the task and answers the children's questions. She asks each child individually if he or she now understands what to do and sends the child to his or her desk.*
9. *Children pick up scissors and cut apart worksheet. They arrange words on their desks. Some students get paper on which to write their sentences. Four students do not write sentences on paper.*
10. *Teacher walks around the room, asking students to read their sentences aloud. She responds to their sentences: laughing at some, praising, commenting on the content, encouraging students to try to arrange the words into another sentence. Periodically, the teacher writes one of the students' sentences on the blackboard.*
11. *After 20 minutes the teacher calls the children to attention and comments that she has seen such excellent sentences on the students' desks that she is very happy with the work they have done. She comments that the sentences she has seen were all very different and that she would like the children to see some of the different sentences composed in the class. She reads nine sentences from the blackboard to the students, commenting on the ideas and the structure of the sentences.*
12. *The teacher asks if any students wish to hand in their papers to her. She tells the students that they may take their sentence papers home if they wish.*

Figure 9 Continued

Teacher's comments:

I wondered if my directions were clear—if I should have used an example of arranging words into sentences with the children when they were assembled on the rug.

Teaching behaviors that seemed to facilitate learning:

1. *Stimulated student interest by providing an example of the desired writing that was appropriate and appealed to the children (two poems).*
2. *Facilitated the children's writing by providing them with words with which to construct sentences. (This overcame the spelling difficulty that the children evidenced at time of last observation.)*
3. *Took the time to be sure that individual children understood the assigned task.*
4. *Took a sincere interest in each child's work as she moved about the room: laughed at the humor contained in sentences, praised the children's efforts, talked about ideas with one or two children who seemed unsure of themselves.*
5. *Carried paper around with her and invited the children to put their sentences on paper because they were such good sentence, and so forth.*

Teacher's comments:

I was happy with the class and really quite pleasantly surprised with the sentences the children produced.

Teaching behaviors that seemed to impede learning:

1. *Teacher began giving directions before all the children were attending to her.*
2. *Teacher ignored or was unaware of one child who very early tired of the task and was somewhat disruptive in that he called out to children across the room, wandered about the room, and appeared to interfere with other students' on-task behavior.*

Teacher's comments:

I realize that I need to wait *longer and be sure that all children are with me before I go on to give directions, and so forth. I* know *it, but it seems as if so much time is elapsing . . . I get impatient.*

Feedback Conference

With the analysis completed (and the report written, if you decided in advance to write one), you are ready for the feedback conference. Hold the conference as soon as possible after the observation, being sure to allot enough time for the analysis. The conference should probably last about 30 minutes. Shorter conferences will seem rushed, and longer conferences tend to produce fatigue and anxiety. The conference should be held in a private setting without interruptions. Allowing phone calls or visitors to interrupt the flow of discussion suggests to the teacher that other matters have higher priority.

How do you conduct the feedback conference? As noted previously, conference styles are usually categorized as *direct* or *indirect*. The direct style is characterized by advising, criticizing, giving directions. The indirect style is marked by reflective listening, praising, supporting. And, as suggested above, learning-centered supervision uses a problem-solving style, one in which the supervisor plays a collaborative and active role in helping the teacher solve instructional problems. In this problem-solving approach, the supervisor acts almost like a second brain for the teacher—probing the problems, recalling data, posing options, reflecting about likely consequences.

Here are examples of the three styles at work.

Direct:

Teacher: I felt I lost their interest toward the last part of the period.
Supervisor: You did. You kept them sitting still too long and you did most of the talking for the final 20 minutes. You should have changed the type of activity.

Indirect:

Teacher: I felt I lost their interest toward the last part of the period.
Supervisor: You're concerned that they weren't really involved.
Teacher: Yes, very much. It's happened before with this class.
Supervisor: You seem to be struggling with your feelings about them as a class. How do you feel about them as a group?

Problem-Solving:

Teacher: I felt I lost their interest toward the last part of the period.
Supervisor: My notes indicate that about half an hour into the period their attention did fall off appreciably. What do you think might have accounted for that?
Teacher: Well, it was a hot, stuffy day. I'm sure that was a factor.
Supervisor: Probably. But it was just as hot the day before, and they seemed more attentive then. What made the difference?
Teacher: You're right. The day before they were busy most of the period doing things. There was a lot of activity, I guess.

The *direct supervisor* advises. The *indirect supervisor* listens. The *problem-solving supervisor* offers data, helps the teacher think about explanations, confronts discrepancies. The problem-solving style is the most difficult of the three to master; but my experience suggests that in the long run, it is the most effective. It respects the teacher as a competent adult able to direct his or her own learning. It involves the teacher in making decisions about future behavior based on an analysis or previous performance. It helps the teacher become responsible for his or her own choices. Yet it also gives the supervisor an active, collaborative role in providing data, reflecting about causes, diagnosing conditions, and finding solutions.

While the problem-solving conference does not follow a rigid formula, it seems most effective when it moves through five sequential stages:

1. *Discerning feelings.* You help the teacher discern the prevailing feelings about the lesson under discussion. Begin at the feeling level, since the feelings about the lesson will yield some important insights about the teacher's perceptions. These feelings will often be of a general sort: "I really feel good about that class," or "I really messed up that period."

2. *Recalling interactions.* Next, move to the specific level by helping the teacher recall a specific part of the class session that gave rise to the positive or negative feelings discerned: "Is there one particular part of the lesson that you remember especially well?"

3. *Analyzing causes.* Now you review the data. You help the teacher analyze the causes of those desirable or undesirable interactions. "My data also suggest that there was much off-task behavior then. Do you remember what you were discussing at that particular point?"

4. *Identifying strategies.* On the basis of that analysis, you help the teacher to identify successful strategies that should be repeated—or to think of alternative strategies that might be used in the future: "If you had put them in small groups, as you suggest, what effect might that have had?"

5. *Generalizing learning.* You help the teacher reflect about the general principles learned from the foregoing analyses. You want the teacher to be able to develop some personal insights that transcend the particular, which can provide useful guidelines for future practice: "What do you think you've learned about handling that mid-period letdown?"

Experienced supervisors, of course, will vary this pattern so that it does not become just one more routine. Simply keep in mind the basic goal: to help the teacher solve a problem and learn from the problem-solving activity.

Formative Assessment Conference

The formative assessment conference is not a time to rate the teacher; it is instead a time to mutually assess what has happened in the past and what should happen in the future. The agenda is a rather simple one:

1. How do the supervisor and the teacher feel about the supervisory *relationship*? Are there any problems relating to their personal interactions? Are any changes desired?

2. How do the supervisor and the teacher feel about the supervisory *process*? Was the frequency of conferences and observations satisfactory? Did the conferences and observations seem productive? Are any changes desired?

3. How do the supervisor and the teacher feel about the teacher's *professional growth*? In what particular ways has the teacher made the most progress? How was that progress attained?

4. How do the supervisor and the teacher feel about the *improvement needed*? What skills still need further development? What specific plan might be developed to bring about those improvements and develop those skills? What other resources are available to the teacher?

5. What have the supervisor and teacher *learned together* about teaching and learning?

In each case the emphasis is on a shared, collaborative interchange in which a spirit of partnership is encouraged.

Implementing Clinical Supervision

Chapter 7 discusses in detail a process for implementing the differentiated system. However, it might be useful at this time to focus on two questions as they relate to clinical supervision. Who should receive it? Who should provide it?

1. *Who should receive clinical supervision?* In the differentiated system, the following groups of teachers should probably receive clinical supervision:

• Inexperienced teachers who are new to teaching. They are still learning the craft of teaching and need a skillful supervisor during those first critical years.

• Experienced teachers who have just begun to teach at a particular school. They are unknown quantities—and should at least begin with clincial supervision until the supervisor is assured of their basic competence.

- Experienced teachers who are encountering serious problems of teaching and learning. They need the intensive help that clinical supervision can provide.
- Competent, experienced teachers who believe they can profit from intensive supervision. Even these teachers can learn from effective supervision—but, for them, clinical supervision should be an option that they choose.

2. *Who should provide clinical supervison?* This answer is more complex. Ideally, a trained supervisor, not an administrator, should provide the clinical supervision. Most administrators are required to evaluate, and experts in the field of supervision seem to agree that the evaluator should not supervise. The evaluation process tends to close off communication between the evaluator and the teacher, making the teacher guarded and reluctant to discuss problems. And effective supervision requires open communication.

However, in many smaller school systems there are no trained supervisors available, and other answers must be found. Several Washington, D.C., schools have developed and implemented a system whereby classroom teachers are trained to act as clinical supervisors for their colleagues. Freeman, Palmer, and Ferren (1980) report that the program has been successful in giving experienced teachers the skills they need to supervise—and in providing good clincial supervision to all who require it.

A second solution is to designate one administrator as chiefly responsible for clinical supervision, without evaluation duties—and to designate another administrator as responsible for evaluation. This solution seems feasible if there are enough administrators available to allow for this role differentiation—and if they can be given the training they need.

A third solution, a variation of the second, is recommended by Sturges and his colleagues (1978). After analyzing the role conflict inherent in supervision, they recommend establishing two supervisory categories: the *administrative supervisor* to evaluate, and the *consultative supervisor* to supervise in the helping sense. Obviously, at a time when districts are reducing supervisory staffs, the implementation of this solution hardly seems feasible.

Another possibility is for neighboring schools to "exchange" principals for consultative supervision. The principal of School A might serve as the clinical supervisor for a few teachers in School B, and School B's principal could do the same for a group of teachers in School A.

A final solution, of course, is for the school principal to attempt to do both jobs of supervising and evaluating. Our research indicates that principals of smaller schools who have established a climate of trust and openness are moderately successful in wearing first one hat and then another, saying, in effect, "All my visits will be supervisory until I tell you otherwise."

So clinical supervision is needed—by a small group of teachers. And it can be effective, if it is provided by a trained supervisor who is not expected also to evaluate.

CHAPTER

3

Cooperative Professional Development

One supervisory option that should be offered to competent, experienced teachers is *cooperative professional development*—a process of collegial collaboration for the improvement of instruction. This chapter describes the nature of cooperative professional development, explains several different approaches to it, reviews the arguments for and against this option, reviews the research relating to it, and indicates how it usually operates within the differentiated model.

The Nature of Cooperative Professional Development

Cooperative professional development is a moderately formalized process by which two or more teachers agree to work together for their own professional growth, usually by observing each other's classes, giving each other feedback about the observation, and discussing shared professional concerns. Often in the literature it is referred to as *peer supervision* or *collegial supervision*. However, these terms seem unfortunate for two reasons. First, our research has shown that teachers often equate the concept of supervision with such negative images as giving orders and making evaluations. Consequently, they are reluctant to participate in any project that suggests that they are "supervising" each other. Second, these terms are misleading; the systems of cooperative or collegial development described in the literature actually provide very few of the supervisory functions identified by experts in the field. And, as Alfonso and Goldsberry (1982) astutely point out, "A clear distinction must be made between the contributions of teachers to the improvement of instruction and the act of supervision as a formal, organizational expectation" (p. 94).

As will be noted below, cooperative professional development can take many forms—from modest programs of two or three exchanges of observations to very ambitious and comprehensive projects in which teams of teachers collaborate in several aspects of the instructional function. In this work, the term is used for any program that has these features:

1. The relationship is moderately formalized and institutionalized. It is not simply an informal exchange of an occasional visit by two or more teachers who are close associates.

2. At a minimum the teachers agree to observe each other's classes at least twice and to hold conferences after those visits.

3. The relationship is among peers. Although an administrator or supervisor may be involved in organizing and occasionally monitoring the program, the observations, conferences, and discussions involve only teachers.

4. The relationship is nonevaluative. It is intended to complement, not take the place of, standard evaluation systems. None of the observation or conference data are shared with administrators or made part of the evaluation process.

These four characteristics define, then, the essential nature of cooperative professional development. As will be noted below, that definition is broad enough to encompass several different variations.

Varieties of Cooperative Professional Development

Such systems of cooperative development, of course, are not new. In 1958, McGuire and his colleagues implemented a somewhat formalized program of intra-school visitation at the University of Chicago Laboratory School. Although the participating teachers reported difficulty in finding time for the observations, they also noted several important benefits: a chance to share teaching methods; a positive reinforcement for aspects of their own teaching; an increased appreciation for their colleagues' work; and an increased understanding of their students.

In the intervening years, peer supervision—or cooperative professional development—has attracted the attention of other educators only sporadically and briefly, for reasons that will be noted below. In the process of its development, however, it has assumed several distinct forms.

1. *Peers as informal observers and consultants.* In what might be termed the standard version of cooperative professional development, collegial team members simply agree to observe each other's classes, making either an unfocused observation or a focused one, depending on the wishes of the teacher being observed. The teachers then confer, with the observer giving feedback informally and consulting together with the teacher about any concerns the teacher might have. The process is a relatively simple one; it does not pretend to have the intensity or precision of clinical supervision.

2. *Peers as clinical supervisors.* As noted in the previous chapter, the Washington, D.C., school district has for the past several years sponsored a program in which teachers are trained to serve as clinical supervisors for their peers. Freeman, Palmer, and Ferren (1980) report that classroom teachers are now used as instructors in the program, teaching their colleagues the basic clinical supervision model, emphasizing such skills as conferring with a nondirective style, gathering factual data, recognizing teaching patterns, and implementing a peer supervision program. They also report highly positive results: 89 percent had a more positive attitude toward supervision; 98 percent expressed an interest in improving instruction; and 94 percent expressed confidence in the clinical model as an aid to improving instruction.

3. *Peers as focused observers.* In the Teacher Expectations and Student Achievement (TESA) program, teachers are trained to act as focused observers for each other (Kerman, 1979). The program begins with workshops in which the research on teacher interactions with pupils is reviewed and participants are taught how to use the interaction techniques in their classes. After each workshop session, teachers observe each other a minimum of four times, for 30 minutes. While being observed, the teacher attempts to use the specific interaction techniques taught in the workshop. The observer merely records the frequency of the interactions with previously targeted students. The observational data are simply given to the teacher observed, who can review them and draw whatever conclusions seem useful. Kerman reports that the program has been highly successful: at the conclusion

of a three-year study, 2,000 low achievers in the experimental classes showed greater academic gains, less absenteeism, and fewer discipline referrals than those in the control classes.

4. *Peers as inservice directors.* Lawrence and Branch (1978) advocate a somewhat more comprehensive approach, which they call the *peer panel.* These peer panels of three to five members serve primarily to direct the inservice work of the faculty, but, according to the authors, provide four other specific functions: (1) they act as a sounding board for members' self-analysis of needs; (2) they assist each other in analyzing curriculum and instruction—often by observing; (3) they give each other feedback about observations; and (4) they verify each other's inservice accomplishments for the record. Although Lawrence and Branch note that the peer panel approach is supported indirectly by the research on inservice education, they do not provide any direct evidence for its success.

5. *Peers as team teachers and observers.* Most approaches to team teaching are, of course, built upon the expectation that members of a team will observe each other and give each other feedback in at least an informal way. In the Individually Guided Education (IGE) model (Withall and Wood, 1979), however, the observations and feedback are somewhat more formalized and are perceived as an integral part of the system. Each participating teacher asks a colleague to observe the classroom, focusing attention on one particular aspect of teaching important to the one observed. The colleague observes, analyzes the observational data, and gives feedback about the observation and the analysis. Withall and Wood cite research conducted at the Pennsylvania State University, which indicates that after only one or two observations there was a significant increase in commitment to use peer observation and in the perceived ability to use the process to improve professional performance.

Note that all versions of cooperative professional development, while varied in their focus and scope, include the four features noted earlier. Each approach has a moderately formalized process, involves observation and feedback, is based on a collegial relationship, and maintains a nonevaluative emphasis.

The Debate Over Cooperative Professional Development

Cooperative professional development, regardless of the form it takes, has not received general acceptance in the profession. Before reviewing the research on its feasibility and its effects, let's review the arguments.

The Pros

Those advocating cooperative professional development argue from several grounds. First, they point out that teachers prefer to turn to colleagues rather than supervisors for advice—and cooperative professional development tends to legitimize and strengthen this tendency. The most comprehensive review of teachers' preferences for consultation is probably that provided by Holdaway and Millikan (1980). In reviewing four separate studies conducted at the University of Alberta over a ten-year period, they note that teachers more frequently called on colleagues for help and tended to value the advice of colleagues more than the advice of supervisors. This finding is supported as well by the research of DeSauctis and Blumberg (Blumberg, 1980) in their study of teachers' conversations. They discovered that 64 percent of the conversations on professional matters were held with colleagues—and only 23 percent with professional staff personnel and 7 percent with the principal.

A second reason stated by supporters for implementing these programs is that teachers can provide useful feedback to each other, without extensive training and without the use of complex forms—and cooperative professional development is structured to make such feedback occur more regularly and more systematically. Brophy (1979) points out that teachers can learn a great deal about their teaching simply by receiving feedback from a colleague about what occurred in the classroom, and urges teachers to work together with competent, interested colleagues.

Finally, advocates of cooperative professional development point out that such collegial systems are built upon and sustain norms of collegiality—and such norms have been found to be a significant feature of successful schools. Little's (1982) study of four successful and two less successful schools concluded that the presence of such norms was an important characteristic of the successful schools. And Berman and McLaughlin's (1978) review of successful innovations reached generally the same conclusion.

The Cons

These arguments have not convinced the skeptics who tend to question both the desirability and feasibility of collegial systems. Those who question the desirability of the system usually point out that untrained teachers cannot provide the same quality of supervision that trained supervisors can provide; they see supervision as a highly skilled process lying beyond the capabilities of untrained individuals. Lieberman (1972) questions its desirability from a cost-benefit perspective; in advising negotiating teams not to support such programs in the contract, he argues that the cost of providing substitutes to release teachers to observe will not have sufficient payoff. Finally, Alfonso (1977) points out that such systems are not likely to be effective, because the observations and feedback conferences appear as random activities and are not linked to system goals.

And there have been those who, while admitting the possible benefits of cooperative development, question its feasibility. Perhaps the most cogent presentation of such reservations can be found in Alfonso and Goldsberry (1982). While generally sympathetic with the values and goals of the cooperative approach, they very usefully describe some important organizational barriers. First, the bureaucratic structure of the school militates against the success of such programs: the lack of time, the inadequate interactions with colleagues, and the physical structure of the school building all get in the way. Second, they note that the prevailing milieu of the schools is antithetical: schools make teachers independent, not team-oriented; competitive, not cooperative; and isolated, not interacting. Finally, they note that collective bargaining agreements often interfere with the successful implementation of such programs, citing the research reported in Alfonso, Firth, and Neville (1981) that most contracts restrict, rather than support, cooperation and collegiality.

The Research on Cooperative Professional Development

Unfortunately, the research does not provide a definitive answer to the controversy. There are a relatively small number of studies—and most have been modest investigations of feasibility. Those that did concern themselves with the effects of such programs usually analyzed only the attitudes and perceptions of participants, not the effect upon behavior. An exception here is a rather carefully designed study conducted by Nelson, Schwartz, and Schmuck (1974), in which they reached this conclusion about what they termed "collegial supervision":

[collegial supervision] can improve the attitudes and professional interdependence of . . . teachers who receive it. . . . The favorable effects of collegial supervision were strongest in the communication adequacy of the primary team.

All of the studies, however, do offer some useful guidelines for practitioners and do yield some tentative support for implementing cooperative programs.

First, a review of all the feasibility studies conducted by doctoral students working under my direction and by other researchers suggests that the following factors have a strong influence on the success of these programs. (For research conducted at the University of Pennsylvania, see: Shapiro, 1978; Chalker, 1979; Ball, 1981; Beck, 1982; Shields, 1982; Cooper, 1983.)

1. *The attitude of administrators.* If administrators oppose such programs, they are less likely to succeed. If, on the other hand, the administrators advocate them too aggressively, they tend to be viewed with distrust. The best attitude seems to be one of support and endorsement—but not aggressive advocacy.

2. *The attitude of teacher associations.* While teacher associations appear reluctant to make official endorsements of such programs, they have been informed and consulted in the programs that seemed to succeed.

3. *The prevailing school climate.* If good relationships exist between teachers and administrators, the programs have a greater likelihood of success; the programs seem not to have fared well where researchers reported serious conflict or pervasive distrust.

4. *The extent to which the program was monitored.* In most of the successful feasibility studies, the researcher played an active role in soliciting support for the cooperative programs and in monitoring their implementation. There is some evidence that those same programs, which were initially successful during the period when the researcher played an active role, had less support and commitment in subsequent years.

5. *The resources available.* While several studies have demonstrated the feasibility of implementing cooperative programs with very limited resources (see especially the Shields' study), the researchers have pointed out that additional resources would have helped. Time, in particular, is the critical commodity—time to learn the skills needed, time to observe, and time to confer.

Thus, the research in general suggests that when these five factors are positive, implementation is successful. What is known about the effects of such programs? As noted above, most of the research has been limited to studies of the effect of participation on teachers' attitudes. Perhaps a dozen such studies have been conducted, varying a great deal, of course, in the rigor of their design and implementation. In only two of these studies (Chalker, 1970; Muir, 1980) did the researcher report either a negative effect or the absence of any discernible shift in attitudes.

Therefore, it seems safe to conclude that, based on limited research, programs of cooperative professional development are feasible and will have positive effects on the attitudes of participants.

Cooperative Professional Development in the Differentiated System

As is explained more fully in Chapter 7, the specifics of how the differentiated program is to be implemented are to a large measure left open to participants. However, the following general approach has been found to be useful in most schools.

First, a member of the administrative or supervisory staff is given responsibility for organizing the program and informally monitoring its progress. That individual meets with the teachers who have expressed interest in and who are eligible for cooperative professional development. As indicated previously, cooperative development probably should be an option only for competent and experienced teachers; beginning teachers and experienced teachers only marginal in performance probably need the more intensive clinical mode.

The leader and the participants together determine the basic provisions under which the program will operate. They begin by discussing the scope of the cooperative program. Will it be confined to observation and conferring—or will it also include curriculum development, materials preparation, inservice sessions, and the exchange of classes? Based on this discussion, the participants then finalize the arrangements under which the program will operate. At a minimum they usually commit themselves to making at least two observations and to hold a feedback conference after each. Two seems to be the absolute minimum; more would probably be desirable, but teachers usually have trouble finding time to make more than two observations and to hold two conferences. Participants also agree to

submit a brief report simply noting when observations and conferences were held. And finally, they agree that the teacher being observed controls the agenda, specifying in general when the observation
is desired and what kind of observation would be most helpful. Our
experience is that teachers will profit most from the program if they
experience and make both an unfocused and a focused observation.

Each participant is then surveyed to determine which colleagues he
or she wishes to work with in the project; our experience indicates that
two- or three-member teams work best. The interactions in larger
teams tend to become too complex. To simplify the matching process,
participants are asked to list a first, second, and third choice of colleagues. It should be noted here that, when left to their own choices,
teachers usually exercise good judgment. An experienced teacher and
a teacher with only two or three years of experience will often pair off
because they know they can learn from each other's quite different
perspective. A 6th-grade teacher and a kindergarten teacher will pair
off to get a different view of the pupils. And at the secondary level,
interdepartmental matchings are common.

The schedule is often an important factor in forming the teams. If at
all possible, team members should have during a given week one
preparation period in common (to discuss their observations) and at
least one preparation period not in common (so that they can visit each
other without needing a substitute.) For this reason it is administra-
tively prudent to organize at least the cooperative component of the
differentiated program at the end of the school year prior to its initia-
tion, so that the school master schedule can reflect these observing and
conferring needs.

If resources are available and participants are interested, a few
training sessions should then be held to give teachers the skills they
need for cooperative professional development. Desirable skills include how to:

- Make an unfocused observation.
- Analyze data from an unfocused observation.
- Confer after an unfocused observation.
- Make a focused observation.
- Analyze data from a focused observation.
- Confer after a focused observation.

If time is limited, the training sessions should probably be restricted to
the three general skills: *observing, analyzing, conferring.*

At a school where teachers said, "We'll participate—but no after-school meetings," we had moderate success in implementing cooperative programs with only one orientation and training session. But additional sessions would have been desirable. Appendix 1 outlines the goals and components of the program and gives suggestions on how to observe and how to confer.

With the orientation and training completed, the program then begins. Teachers observe, analyze, and confer, submitting a simple progress report. The administrator or supervisor responsible for the program checks the reports and confers informally with participants, just to be sure that the program is moving along well and that problems are dealt with. The main problem is predictable: even teachers with the best of intentions will continue to postpone the observations and the conferences. A few reminders are usually enough to get the program back on track again.

It's a relatively simple, low-key program that doesn't make too many promises or demands. It will probably not bring about significant changes in behavior—but it will raise the level of professional talk, give teachers feedback about a limited part of their teaching, and help them to see their colleagues—and supervision—in a new light.

4

Self-Directed Development

A second option offered to those who do not need or want clinical supervision is termed *self-directed development*, a process in which a teacher works independently, directing his or her own professional growth. This chapter explains more fully the nature of self-directed development, describes some alternative versions of it now in operation, reviews the arguments advanced for and against its use, summarizes the research, and describes in detail how it operates in the differentiated program.

The Nature of Self-Directed Development

As used in the program of differentiated supervision, self-directed development is a process of professional growth characterized by four features:

1. *The individual works independently on a program of professional growth.* Although a member of the leadership team acts as a resource for the teacher, the teacher is not supervised by others, in the conventional sense of that term, and the teacher does not work cooperatively with other members of a team.

2. *The individual develops and follows a goal-oriented program of professional improvement.* The goals of that program stem from the teacher's own assessment of professional need; there is no necessity for

the teacher's goals to be derived from organizational goals. It is assumed that any professional growth will contribute at least indirectly to the school's goals.

3. *The individual has access to a variety of resources in working toward those goals.* Based on the nature of the goals set, the leader and the teacher may decide that one or more of the following resources and experiences might be appropriate: videotapes of the teacher's teaching; feedback from students; professional books and computerized information services; graduate courses and intensive workshops; support from school and district supervisors and administrators; interschool visitation.

4. *The results of the self-directed program are not used in evaluating teacher performance.* The program is entirely divorced from evaluation; it is assumed that the teacher will be evaluated by whatever district program is in place.

These four characteristics distinguish self-directed professional growth both from other components of the differentiated program and from other types of inservice education.

Versions of Self-Directed Development

A careful review of the literature yields relatively few citations on self-supervision, which is perhaps a contradiction in terms, or self-directed professional growth. There are, however, references to two analogous approaches: *self-appraisal systems* and *self-analysis of instruction with videotape.* While each differs in some respects from the self-directed development defined above, perhaps a review of these analogous approaches can shed some light on the strengths and weaknesses of the approach under discussion.

Self-Appraisal Systems

While self-directed professional development is distinctly non-evaluative in nature, it is similar in several other respects to self-appraisal systems, which have been discussed frequently in the professional journals. Since almost all self-appraisal programs are variations of management-by-objective (MBO) systems, the following discussion focuses on this particular version of self-directed development.

How do self-appraisal systems work? While there are some variations in individual plans, in general they seem to follow a somewhat similar process. (For additional detail on representative plans, see Armstrong, 1973; Lewis, 1973; and Redfern, 1980.)

1. Administrators establish district and school goals for the year, which are shared with the supervisory and instructional staff.

2. Each staff member does a self-evaluation and sets individual performance targets, which are expected to be related to district or school goals.

3. Each staff member develops an appraisal contract, listing performance objectives, methods of achieving those objectives, resources needed, and the means by which attainment will be evaluated.

4. Each staff member confers with the administrator-evaluator to review the appraisal contract and to make any modifications deemed necessary.

5. The staff member and the evaluator confer periodically to monitor progress.

6. The staff member and the evaluator hold a summative conference to assess the attainment of the performance targets and to make plans for the next appraisal cycle.

Perhaps the best assessment of how such plans actually work in schools comes from the Hyde Park, New York, school system, which has used an MBO system since 1972. In what seems to be a candid assessment of its strengths and weaknesses, Gray and Burns (1979) conclude that it has achieved mixed success after a somewhat promising beginning: "Through the years . . . the number and quality of job objectives set by teachers and administrators has declined" (p. 415). After reviewing the Hyde Park experience and that of other schools using such plans, they conclude that several factors explain the limited success of MBO appraisal systems:

• There were no sanctions for mediocre performance.

• The ratio of teachers to administrators was too large for effective appraisal.

• The teacher association insisted on restrictive contract provisions.

• There was insufficient staff development to accompany the program.

• Some administrators were too lenient in reviewing performance targets.

• There was often a climate of distrust and suspicion prevalent in the district.

And Iwanicki (1981) adds this observation: "Where MBO-oriented approaches have been implemented, teachers have tended to feel that they were being manipulated or coerced into developing objectives in areas defined by the administration" (p. 205). In response to this perceived weakness, he has developed his own version. Iwanicki's "contract plan" is similar to MBO except that it places more emphasis on self-evaluation and minimizes the role of organizational goals. Yet it is still essentially an appraisal system, which he notes cannot be used to rank teachers. From my perspective, it seems more useful to divorce appraisal from self-improvement—to use self-directed, non-evaluative systems to bring about professional growth; and to use sound appraisal systems for rating teachers.

Self-Analysis of Videotaped Instruction

A second version of self-directed professional development empha-sizes the analyses of videotapes of teachers' classrooms. Although Chapter 6 discusses in detail the use of videotape as a general supervis-ory resource, it seems appropriate here to describe briefly a self-directed program that relies solely on videotape analysis. According to Moritz and Martin-Reynolds (1980), the Maumee, Ohio, school district has developed a program of self-analysis and self-development that makes primary use of a split-screen technique: the teacher is on one half of the screen and the pupils are on the other half. As they describe the process, the teacher begins by presenting a micro-teaching lesson to peers and has a brief practice taping in the classroom, simply to become accustomed to the taping process. The teacher then chooses the class or activity he or she wants taped, and the videotape is made. The teacher next reviews the tape—first, with the audio off to focus on nonverbal behavior—and, second, with the video off, to focus on ver-bal behavior. After viewing and analyzing the tape, the teacher iden-tifies one or two verbal or nonverbal skills that can be improved and that will become the focus of the teacher's development during the month to come. With the analysis completed, the teacher then meets with a supervisor or administrator to share the tape and the results of the self-analysis.

Moritz and Martin-Reynolds recommend that this cycle of taping-goal setting-sharing occur about three or four times the first year the program is in operation, with reduced frequency in subsequent years. Citing a survey of a sample of Ohio teachers over a three-year period, they report that teachers feel positive about the program, prefer vid-eotaped self-evaluation to "traditional" evaluation, and believe that sharing the tape with an administrator was a "non-threatening" experience.

The Arguments For and Against Self-Directed Development

Regardless of the form it takes, self-directed development has not been generally accepted as a model for professional growth. It might be useful to review the arguments here before turning to the research.

Those advocating self-directed development usually argue from three grounds; the individualized needs of teachers, the nature of adult learning, and the professionalism of teaching. They point out, first, that teachers are individuals with very distinct needs and learning styles. Bents and Howey (1981) note, for example, that as adults, teachers are at different stages of development along both the interpersonal and cognitive dimensions. Drawing from the work of Santmire (1979), they point out that some teachers are at a rather basic level of conceptual development. Their learning styles are characterized by these features: they are oriented toward the practical; want to know what is "correct" and what is "incorrect"; prefer learning that is presented or sanctioned by an authority; and prefer to be involved in staff development programs that are clearly organized and systematic. Other teachers, Bents and Howey suggest, are at a somewhat more advanced level of conceptual development, whose preferred learning styles are characterized by quite different features: they tend to question more; are more interested in principles and issues; will sometimes challenge authorities; and prefer group discussion and inquiry to lecture.

The second argument is based on the tenets of adult learning theory. In synthesizing the theory and research on adult learning, Knowles (1978) offers five principles that he considers the "foundation stones" of adult learning theory—and two of these five point directly toward the need for individualizing the professional growth of teachers. First, adults have a deep need to be self-directing; as a consequence, they should be involved in programs that foster such self-direction. Second, individual differences increase with age; adult learning, therefore, should make optimal provisions for differences in style, time, place, and pace of learning. Thus, self-directed programs are more likely to respond to the need for self-direction and to adult developmental differences.

A final argument for self-directed development is based on the professional nature of teaching. Armstrong (1973) points out that teaching has become increasingly professionalized: teachers have assumed quasi-managerial roles, directing the work of aides, para-professionals, student teachers, and volunteers—and taking an increasingly larger role in the decision-making process. Advocates of self-directed learning believe that teachers, as professionals, should be able to judge their own performance.

Others in the profession are not persuaded by these arguments. They note that individual needs can be effectively met in group interactions: the teacher working with a group of colleagues takes from the interactions whatever is needed for professional growth. All learning, in their terms, is individualized since every participant constructs personal meaning from each encounter. Their second argument, in fact, emphasizes the importance of such interactions in learning. Learning at its best is the growth that comes from professional dialogue and encounter; teachers need other teachers and supervisors for stimulation, challenge, and support. Finally, as McNeil and Popham (1973) point out, most teachers are not autonomous, self-directing learners: they lack the capacity to make accurate evaluations of themselves, to identify areas for improvement, and to complete a program of independent study.

So the argument is joined, chiefly on theoretical grounds. What does the empirical evidence suggest?

The Research on Self-Directed Development

Since there is relatively little research that explicitly examines programs of self-directed development, the brief review that follows examines instead the assumptions that undergird such programs. Based on the studies available, the following tentative conclusions can provide a useful guide to action.

1. *Teachers do not seem to be able to make reliable appraisals of their own teaching.* In reviewing the research on self-appraisal, Carroll (1981) concludes, "Empirical studies have generally demonstrated that self-ratings show little agreement with ratings of students, colleagues, or administrators" (p. 181). He cites studies that indicate that, while the correlation between self-ratings and student ratings was

only .28, the correlation between student ratings and colleague ratings was .70.

2. *Teacher reports of their classroom behaviors tend not to correspond with the reports of observers.* After reviewing several studies that compare teacher's reports of what went on in their classrooms with the reports of observers who were present, Hook and Rosenshine (1979) conclude, ". . . one is not advised to accept teacher reports of specific behaviors as particularly accurate. No slur is intended; teachers do not have practice in estimating their behavior and then checking against actual performance" (p. 10).

3. *Feedback to the teacher by means of videotape is most effective when another observer is present during the viewing to present a second point of view and to focus the teacher's attention.* Based on their review of the research on feedback by video, Fuller and Manning (1973) conclude that the presence of an observer to focus and confront is highly desirable.

4. *Teachers can learn from self-instructional materials as well as they can learn from supervision or course instructors.* Several studies support the use of self-instructional materials by mature learners. Edwards (1975) concluded that students who did their micro-teaching with self-instructional materials—and without a supervisor—performed just as well as those who used the self-instructional materials with a supervisor's help. And in a meta-analysis of 75 studies comparing the use of the Keller Personalized System of Instruction (which emphasizes independent and self-paced learning) with conventional classroom instruction, Kulik, Kulik, and Cohen (1980) concluded that college students using such systems had higher examination scores and gave their courses higher ratings, without increasing the amount of study time.

5. *Individualized staff development programs tend to be more effective than those that present uniform experiences to all participants.* Lawrence's (1974) review of 97 studies of inservice programs concluded that programs with individualized activities were more likely to achieve their objectives than those that provided similar experiences for all participants.

The research tends to suggest, then, that there is merit in both positions. Teachers can acquire some skills and information from independent learning and will prefer programs that provide some choice of activities—but their professional growth will be better facilitated if they have feedback from sources other than their own perceptions and can work with someone who can focus their learning.

Self-Directed Development in the Differentiated Model

Self-directed development in the differentiated model attempts to build upon the strengths of several individualized approaches to professional growth—while trying to avoid the pitfalls of each.

As with the cooperative program, one administrator or supervisor is expected to provide leadership in this component. Our pilot studies indicate that the principal can often play this role successfully, although an assistant principal, district supervisor, or school supervisor might also have the requisite skills. This designated leader meets with all the teachers interested in and eligible for the self-directed component. Again, our experience suggests that beginning teachers and experienced teachers with problems should be directed into the clinical component, since the self-directed mode seems to work best for mature and competent teachers.

At this initial meeting, the following issues should be resolved through open discussion:

• *To what extent should the teacher's plan for professional growth be formalized?* Our pilot studies indicate that the program works best when teachers are asked to develop and submit a relatively simple proposal for their self-directed development. Some structure is needed—without making the process seem too bureaucratic.

• *What resources will be available for the self-directed component?* It is important at the outset to specify the range of resources available—and the fiscal and time constraints that operate. Participants need to know to what extent they will be able to make use of resources such as the following: videotape; student feedback; professional books and computerized information sources; collegial consultation; supervisor and administrator assistance; observations within and outside the school; graduate courses, special workshops, and inservice programs; professional travel and conference attendance.

• *What type of monitoring will be anticipated?* While self-directed development excludes the evaluation process, it does need to be monitored by a supervisor or administrator. Brief and informal conferences are sufficient for this purpose—but the matter needs to be resolved at the outset.

Each teacher involved, then, is expected to develop a plan for self-directed development. Our experience suggests that a simple proposal is best. On the form the teacher should first indicate one or two goals for professional development. In contrast to the advocates of **MBO** approaches, who insist on measurable objectives, I believe that it is more useful to encourage teachers to set goals for themselves without worrying about whether the goal is quantifiable, measurable, or precisely stated. McGreal (1983) notes that teachers and supervisors will accept the goal-setting process more readily if it is made clear that the judgments made by trained and experienced teachers and supervisors are valid measures.

As an example of the types of goals that might be posed, consider the following, which were developed by teachers in our pilot studies:

- To become more knowledgeable about the composing process—and to make use of the process in my classroom.
- To learn how to teach critical thinking in my 4th-grade science lessons.
- To become more skilled in questioning pupils and responding to their answers.
- To find out more about moral development in the classroom.
- To develop materials to stimulate pupils' creativity.

The teacher then indicates on the form a tentative plan of action for achieving the stated goals. Again, this plan of action can be stated generally. It simply helps the teacher to consider some specific steps that can be taken toward accomplishment of the goal. The final component of the proposal asks the teacher to note the personal and material resources needed.

These self-directed development proposals are then submitted to the leader in charge of this component of the program, who confers with each participant individually. The purposes of this conference are simply to be sure the goal is clearly understood by both leader and teacher, to exchange ideas about the action plan, and to agree on the resources that will be committed. It is not expected that the leader will attempt to persuade the teacher to propose another goal; self-directed development is based on the primacy of personal, not organizational, goals.

Next, the teacher begins to work on the plan for self-directed development, conferring from time to time with the leader about progress and problems. Although the teacher will for the most part be working independently, it is expected that the designated leader will play an active role as a resource for the teacher—suggesting sources, exchanging ideas, reflecting with the teacher about issues, and providing support throughout the program. Since there is no evaluation associated with self-directed development, it enables the administrator or supervisor to play the role of supportive and resourceful colleague.

At the end of the year the teacher and the leader then confer again to review what has been accomplished. The conference is primarily a time for the teacher to reflect about what has been learned—without worrying unduly about what has *not* been accomplished. The leader plays the role of a reflective listener, helping the teacher probe the meaning of the entire experience for the teacher's personal and professional growth.

Not all teachers will want this mode of growth. It does place a high premium on autonomy and independence. But for those who do, our studies indicate that it can be a very meaningful substitute for clinical supervision.

5

Administrative
Monitoring

Administrative monitoring may be a new term—but it's an old practice. The term is used in this book to describe what some call
"drop-in supervision"—the brief and informal observations by a principal or assistant principal. This chapter explains how such observations can be an effective part of the differentiated program.

At the outset it might be useful to clarify the relationship between
administrative monitoring and the other components of the program—and to review the limited literature on the subject.

The Nature of Administrative Monitoring

In the differentiated program, administrative monitoring can either
be an option for those not participating in clinical supervision—or it
can be provided for all teachers as a complement to the other components. In some schools in which I have worked as a consultant, the
principal in effect has said to the teachers, "If you don't need clinical
supervision—and you don't want either the cooperative or self-directed mode, then you get administrative monitoring." In other
schools the principal has said, "Everyone gets administrative
monitoring; in addition, you choose one of the other three." Both
patterns seem to work. The choice seems to depend on the size of the
school, the size of the administrative staff, and the principal's leadership style.

The Research on Administrative Monitoring

How effective is administrative monitoring? The answers are somewhat contradictory. First, brief and informal visits by an administrator are obviously not likely to change a teacher's behavior. No planning precedes the observation; the observer does not remain long enough to note patterns of behavior; and there is usually no follow-up conference. Because such visits are ineffective in changing behavior and suggest to some an attitude of distrust, the practice is usually dismissed by consultants, professors of supervision, and writers in the field.

However, it is an approach sanctioned by the advice and practice of experienced school administrators. One principal put it this way:

> *I get to every classroom at least once a week. And I don't care what the experts say—I know it makes a difference. I pick up a lot of information about what is going on. I've learned how to smell problems from those very brief visits. I see teachers doing good things. Teachers know I care about learning because I'm in the classroom. The kids know I'm not hiding in my office. It just seems to keep everybody on their toes.*

And, perhaps surprisingly, the research now suggests that those experienced principals knew what they were doing. Several reviews of the research on effective schools (see, for example, Squires, Huitt, and Segars, 1981) conclude that in effective schools, the principal is a highly visible leader who frequently monitors the classroom, stays well informed about daily life in the school, and demonstrates an interest in instruction by spending much time in instructional settings—all of which imply the use of administrative monitoring.

Characteristics of Administrative Monitoring

1. *Administrative monitoring should be open.* The principal should discuss openly with the staff these important issues that will probably concern the teachers being observed:

• Who will do the monitoring? As the term implies, it is best done by a school administrator, not a supervisor. Since it is essentially an administrative function and its intent is not solely supervisory (in the sense of helping teachers improve instruction), it is more appropriately carried out by a principal or assistant principal.

- What kind of behavior can the teacher typically expect from the administrator who drops in for a monitorial visit? Some principals like their presence to be acknowledged; others prefer that the teacher continue with instruction without acknowledging the visitor's presence. Some principals like to speak briefly with the pupils, especially in less formal elementary classrooms; others prefer simply to observe. These matters should be discussed so that both teacher and administrator are clear about these expectations.

- What kind of feedback may the teacher expect after a drop-in visit? Anyone who is observed even briefly has some anxiety about the impressions of the observer and appreciates some kind of feedback, even if it is only a few words of commendation. Therefore, it is recommended that the principal give the teacher feedback in a systematic fashion. Regardless of the decision, however, the matter should be discussed.

- What records will be kept of the monitoring? The observer should probably make brief notes about each visit, and should assure the teachers that these notes are available for their review, if they have any anxiety about the matter.

- Will data from monitorial observations be made part of the evaluation process? This is a sensitive issue, which needs to be discussed candidly. Even though the formal evaluation of teacher performance should be based primarily on carefully structured and implemented observations, the fact that data from monitorial visits will inevitably influence the administrator's judgment should be acknowledged. A statement of this sort usually suffices:

> In the administrative monitoring, I'll be visiting your classes briefly, primarily to keep informed about teaching and learning on a day-to-day basis. I will not be making formal evaluations of your teaching; those formal evaluations will occur in evaluation visits. However, I will be forming impressions of your work, and making brief notes about my visit. If at any time my brief observations suggest that some serious problems exist, you may be assured that I will let you know directly.

2. *Administrative monitoring should be planned and scheduled, not done randomly and unsystematically.* The administrator should begin by blocking out time in the weekly schedule. It is also useful to develop a monitoring schedule that will yield some systematic observation. There are various ways to approach the monitoring process.

- Many effective principals monitor *at crucial times* in the school day: when school begins, during lunch periods, and at the end of the day.
- Some principals monitor *grade by grade,* visiting all 6th-grade classrooms in a given week, for example. Thus, in a few days' time they will have gotten a bird's-eye view of what's going on in a particular grade.
- Other principals monitor *subject by subject,* visiting all mathematics classes during a given week, for example. In this way they get a cross-section of mathematics teaching and learning across the school.
- Still others prefer to get *a series of contrastive snapshots:* how is English for the gifted different from English for college-preparatory students—and how is that different from English for the less able?

If monitoring is planned and systematic, the administrator will be able, in a relatively brief period of time, to get a somewhat reliable picture of teaching and learning in that school. If a principal can make four such visits in a 45-minute period (counting the time required to go from room to room) and can set aside even one period a day, then in a week's time he or she will have observed 20 classrooms—a rather representative sample, if the visiting has been carefully planned.

3. *Administrative monitoring should be learning-centered.* Since the monitorial visit will be brief, it is essential to focus only on the critical aspects of learning—and how teaching has facilitated or impeded that learning. By concentrating on the following key questions, the observer is able to maintain a learning-centered focus, avoid distractions, and make the most of a brief visit.

- What model of learning and teaching is the teacher attempting to implement? Is this a discovery or an inquiry lesson, a direct instruction presentation, or a creative arts workshop?
- How many pupils are on-task and how many seem off-task? To what extent does the teacher seem aware of and responsive to off-task behavior? What behaviors of other pupils and the teacher appear to be contributing to the off-task behavior?
- To what extent do pupils seem aware of and involved with the learning objectives? How many pupils at a given point in time seem to be actively participating in learning? What is the teacher doing to facilitate or impede such participation?
- What kind of feedback are pupils getting about their learning? Are they sufficiently aware of progress and problems? What is the teacher doing to facilitate such awareness?

4. *Administrative monitoring is likely to be most effective when it is interactive across two dimensions: the administrator gives feedback to the teacher and uses the observational data as part of an ongoing assessment of the instructional program and the school climate.* As noted above, the teacher should receive feedback of both a positive and negative sort, as appropriate. The observer should reinforce an effective teacher behavior with praise: "I like the way you monitored the small-group discussions." Less effective behavior should be questioned: "I felt some concern about the fact that pupils in the back of the room seemed inattentive. What was your perception?"

And the wise administrator uses the observations to monitor the school on a day-to-day basis:

- Are there certain times during the day when pupils seem inattentive and disruptive in class?
- Are there certain places in the building where pupils seem easily distracted?
- How much direct instruction goes on across grades, ability levels, and subjects?
- Is it used excessively, insufficiently, or inappropriately?
- To what extent are teachers giving attention to critical thinking and the higher thought processes?
- How much do teachers vary content and method from group to group?

Answers to such questions can point to problems that will need more systematic examination and analysis.

Implementation of Administrative Monitoring

How should administrative monitoring be implemented in the differentiated approach? While some answers have just been suggested, it might be appropriate at this point to describe the process more explicitly.

First, the leadership team decides who will monitor. As noted earlier, this should be the responsibility of an administrator, preferably one at the school, not the district, level. The team, with input from the instructional staff, then decides whether administrative monitoring is to be offered only as an option for those choosing it—or is to be provided to all teachers, who then choose one of the other modes in addition to the monitoring.

The administrator responsible for the monitoring then meets with all those who will be involved—either those choosing it as an option or the entire faculty. The issues noted earlier are discussed and resolved: the person responsible; the observer's behavior as a visitor; the nature of the feedback process; the records to be kept; and the relationship to evaluation. The administrator then develops a monitoring schedule for his or her use only. The schedule should probably not be shared with the teachers, since the intent is to get representative pictures of unrehearsed behavior.

Then the visits begin. The administrator stays in a class for five to ten minutes—just long enough to get a sense of what learning and teaching are going on. The observer focuses on the key elements cited earlier: the learning-teaching model; on-task and off-task behavior; awareness of and involvement with objectives; and nature and source of feedback about learning. The observer leaves, giving the teacher a nonverbal signal or a brief word of appreciation for the opportunity to visit.

Upon leaving, it is probably useful for the administrator to make a brief note of the observation, while impressions are still vivid. I find a 4×6 index card useful for recording both the basic information (date, time, teacher observed, type of class) and observational notes on the key learning and teaching elements. Figure 10 illustrates these points.

The administrator should then give the teacher some immediate feedback about the observation. If at all possible, the feedback should be given in a face-to-face exchange: a brief discussion between classes, at lunch, or at the end of the day. If such oral feedback is not always feasible, then a brief note will do. Regardless of the form of the interaction, the observer should always try to find something positive to commend; and, if there were problems, the feedback should probably be confined to only one question or concern.

Figure 10. Notes from Administrative Monitoring

oct 10, pd 2   *Loren Jones, 10th-grade English*

Small-group discussions on Frost poem.
Jones sitting with one group; about one-third of pupils in other groups seem off-task. J. seems unaware of them.
In groups where I checked, pupils seem unclear about their task; no one seemed to be acting as leader for groups. In each group one pupil seemed to dominate discussion.

J. Walker

If a brief conference is held, then obviously a more direct style is called for, since time is limited. So the principal might say to Mr. Jones after the visit recorded in Figure 10:

> *Thanks for the chance to drop by this morning. I liked your use of small groups in discussing poetry. Several of the pupils had a chance to talk about the poem—and they seemed interested in it. I did have a concern about the groups you were not sitting with. Several seemed unclear about the purpose of the discussion. What were your perceptions?*

A brief note would have the same content: always one positive comment—and one concern, if problems existed.

Good principals have always monitored. Administrative monitoring can perhaps be a more effective practice if the guidelines in this chapter are kept in mind.

CHAPTER

6

Resources for Differentiated Supervision

In all of these supervisory modes, professional colleagues obviously play a central role: a trained supervisor is essential for clinical supervision; peers are vital in the cooperative mode; a supervisor or principal can best facilitate self-directed development; and an astute administrator must monitor. However, there are three other special resources that can be used in the clinical, cooperative, and self-directed supervisory modes: *student feedback, videotape analysis,* and *the reflective journal.* Each in its own way can supplement the assistance of the professional colleague.

Student Feedback

Over the past several years there has been much debate about the usefulness of student ratings of teachers. Those who question the value of such ratings usually make the following arguments: students are too immature to evaluate teaching; students can best evaluate a teacher only after several years have elapsed to give them a needed perspective; student rating forms are neither reliable nor valid; and student rating systems are actually popularity contests.

Those advocating the use of student ratings usually turn to the research to support their counterclaims. However, as Aleamoni (1981) notes, "Most of the research and use of the student rating forms has occurred at the college and university level. Generalizations to other educational and noneducational levels will be left to the discretion of the reader" (p. 110). Given that caution, his review of the research on student ratings of teachers does provide some tentative empirical grounds for resolving the issue. These findings seem most useful:

1. Students tend to make consistent ratings from one year to the next. Correlations between student ratings of the same course and instructor range from .70 to .87.

2. Students appear to be discriminating judges. In several studies they have been able to make distinctions between an instructor's personal qualities and his or her professional competence.

3. Student judgments seem not to change over time. Ratings of alumni who had been out of school for five to ten years were consistent with those of students currently enrolled.

4. Well-developed forms and procedures tend to yield both reliable and valid results. Aleamoni cautions, however, that most rating forms developed by students and faculty without the aid of professionals tend to produce unreliable results.

5. The research is inconclusive as to whether student ratings can improve instruction. However, two relatively recent studies (Aleamoni, 1978; McKeachie, 1979) concluded that instructors made significant improvements in their ratings when personal consultations were provided.

These findings on the usefulness of student ratings at the college level are supported by just a few studies at the elementary and secondary level. After reviewing several reports of student ratings of elementary and secondary teachers, Shaw (1973) noted that an increasing number of school districts were using student evaluations. Based on her review of those reports, she made the following recommendations to those contemplating the use of student ratings: (1) make such programs voluntary for teachers at the beginning; (2) provide strong administrative leadership in initiating the program but involve teachers extensively in developing forms and procedures; and (3) make clear at the outset whether student ratings will be used as part of the formal evaluation system. And Bryan (1966) found that teachers who used the Teacher Image Questionnaire changed their teaching after studying their profiles yielded from student responses. Additional support for the use of student feedback can be found in Anderson and Walberg's (1974) research; they note that several studies demonstrate that students can make reliable observations of the classroom learning environment—and point out that such environmental measures are valid predictors of learning.

Since the research on student evaluation of elementary and secondary teachers is not conclusive, and since teachers' associations for the most part strongly resist their mandated use, it would seem unwise to make such ratings a required part of any supervisory program. However, our experience suggests that teachers will accept student feedback as a resource if three conditions exist.

First, the use of student feedback should be optional in the differentiated program. Those responsible for leading the differentiated program should review with teachers the research on student feedback and simply note that it is one useful resource for improving teaching—not a required part of the program. Second, teachers should be assured that they control access to the results. If a teacher decides to secure student feedback, then that teacher decides whether to share the results with peers, supervisors, or administrators. Finally, it should be made clear that student feedback will not be used in the formal evaluation of teaching performance.

If student feedback is provided as an optional resource, those involved can decide either to use a standardized form or to develop their own. Since the results from student feedback will not be used in the evaluation of teaching, there is less need to be concerned about the use of homemade forms.

Three types of homemade forms can be developed. One alternative is to develop a *general* form that uses simple language to ask about the essential components of good teaching. Those involved should review the research on teacher effectiveness, choose the skills and attributes they wish to assess, and then phrase those skills without professional jargon. One such form is illustrated in Figure 11.

A second type of homemade form is *subject-specific*. Teachers in a specific subject area meet, review the research on teaching and learning in their discipline, and then develop a form that focuses on the important skills in teaching that discipline—or one phase of it. Figure 12 shows a sample form for teachers who want feedback from students about the teaching of writing.

The third type of student feedback *focuses on the learning environment*, not the teacher. These forms ask students for their perceptions of the learning environment, with the items phrased so that the focus is away from the teacher. For example, "I have a chance to express my ideas in this class." McGreal (1983) makes the point that such feedback has three distinct advantages over feedback about the teacher: it is likely to be more accurate and consistent; it is likely to be better accepted by teachers; and it is formative, not summative, in nature.

Figure 11. General Form for Obtaining Student Feedback

Directions: Your teacher would like to know how you feel about his or her teaching in your class. Read each sentence below. Decide how true it is about your teacher. Circle one of the four choices in front of each sentence. The choices are:

    F = very much false
    f = more false than true
    t = more true than false
    T = very much true

This teacher:

F f t T   keeps us busy for the whole period.

F f t T   knows how to have good discipline in our class.

F f t T   explains ideas clearly.

F f t T   makes us want to do our best work.

F f t T   is fair with everybody and does not play favorites.

F f t T   makes our school work seem interesting.

F f t T   tells us each day what we are supposed to learn.

F f t T   grades our tests and papers fairly.

F f t T   helps us practice what we have learned.

F f t T   is always friendly with students.

One of the values of such homemade forms is that they stimulate and motivate professional dialogue. As teachers discuss the qualities of effective teaching and decide which aspects they wish to assess, they value and profit from the exchange of views.

Videotape Analysis

A second optional resource that should be made available to those using the clinical, cooperative, or self-directed modes is the guided analysis of videotapes of the teacher's own classroom. As with student feedback, those participating should have some very specific assurances about the following matters: the teacher will decide which class will be taped; the teacher will control access to the tape; and the tape will not be used as part of the formal evaluation of teaching.

A review of the research on the use of videotape (see Fuller and Manning, 1973, for a comprehensive summary) and an analysis of my

Figure 12. Subject-Specific Form for Obtaining Student Feedback:
The Teaching of Writing

Directions: Your English teacher is interested in finding out what you think about how writing is taught in your English class. Read each sentence below. Decide how true it is about how your teacher teaches writing. Circle one of the four choices in front of each statement. The choices are:

F = very much false
f = more false than true
t = more true than false
T = very much true

This teacher:

F f t T   helps us get ideas for our writing.

F f t T   lets us choose our own topics.

F f t T   helps us publish class magazines and newspapers.

F f t T   teaches us how to plan and organize our writing.

F f t T   lets us work in groups to get help from each other.

F f t T   shows us how to revise our writing to make it better.

F f t T   gives us time in class to revise our writing.

F f t T   teaches us the skills we need to write well.

F f t T   grades our writing fairly.

F f t T   praises our writing when it is good.

own experience in using it with teachers and supervisors suggest that the following system will result in most effective use.

1. The teacher chooses the class to be taped, keeping in mind Fuller and Manning's suggestion that the session should be a typical, not an unusual, one. The teacher and the consultant (*consultant* is used here to refer to a supervisor, administrator, or a peer with special training) discuss what teacher or pupil behaviors might provide the best focus for the taping. For example, they may decide that the teacher's responses to student answers might be an appropriate focus. They develop a form for their use in examining more closely this aspect of teaching, if there is time and if they agree that such a form would be useful. In this case the teacher might prepare a seating chart for the class to be taped, along with a simple code indicating how the teacher responded to answers from each student:

R = Repeated answer.
P = Responded positively to answer.
N = Responded negatively to answer.
S = Asked other students to evaluate answer or to answer question.
U = Used the answer in moving discussion forward.
I = Seemed to ignore or make no response to answer.

2. The taping is arranged for and carried out, usually by a trained student or technician, who has been briefed about the professional focus of the taping, since that might affect the technical aspects of the taping.

3. The teacher first views the tape alone. If a form was developed for the skill under examination, the teacher may use the form independently during this solo viewing. If no form was developed, then the teacher is simply instructed to focus on the behaviors identified. At this time the teacher may decide not to share the tape with the consultant; and the teacher is assured that there is no need to give a reason for such a decision.

4. If the teacher decides to share the tape with the consultant, the consultant should have an opportunity to view the tape alone, in order to analyze the tape systematically and objectively, without being influenced by the presence of the teacher. It is difficult to analyze a tape with an anxious teacher nearby.

5. The teacher and the consultant then arrange to view the tape together. Again the focus is on the particular behavior that they had agreed to examine—using either the special form or simply by looking closely at the behavior. The consultant plays a crucial role here. He or she should be supportive and empathetic, calling attention to strengths and empathizing with the teacher's feelings. However, the consultant must also be prepared to confront—noting discrepancies between the teacher's perceptions and the consultant's observations. Fuller and Manning recommend here—and the recommendation seems like a wise one—that the consultant call attention to *moderate* discrepancies, avoiding those that might be either too minor to note or too threatening to deal with.

Our experience with schools in the pilot studies indicates that teachers who at first seem reluctant to have their classes videotaped find it a very valuable experience if they have the support and advice of a skilled consultant.

The Reflective Journal

The reflective journal is a personal record and account of the teacher's experiences, feelings, and reactions during the supervisory process. As such it has primary value for those working in the self-directed mode, although it can also be used successfully by those experiencing the clinical or the cooperative approach.

As a means of recording and reflecting about one's experiences, the personal journal, of course, has had a long and honored history. Writers like Henry Thoreau and mystics like Thomas Merton have attested to its value, and many English teachers have advocated its use with students. Only recently, however, has the journal been used systematically with teachers as a way of helping them reflect about and grow from their professional experience. As far as I can determine, Yinger and Clark (1981) are the first to provide a well-documented account of the use of the journal as a resource for staff development. They report that the journal is a useful means for facilitating teacher reflection and analysis. Others in the profession, however, have used variations of the journal as a means of facilitating teacher growth. Ryan (1981) suggests that teachers should be encouraged to tell their personal stories, either to a trained story collector or to a sympathetic listener. And Perrone (1977) recommends the use of teacher recollections as a means of evaluating programs and helping teachers grow professionally.

My own experience in using journals with both students and teachers indicates that there are two personality types who do not appear to profit from journal keeping: (1) the *unreflective*, who seem content to live on the surface of life—they seem unaware of the depths of experience; and (2) the *troubled*, who are deeply disturbed and anxious about aspects of their personal and professional lives—they are afraid of what they might find at the center. Asked to keep a journal, both the unaware and the afraid turn the journal into a diary of the trivial: persons met, appointments kept, and chores accomplished.

For this reason the reflective journal should be an option, not a requirement, for teachers experiencing the clinical, the cooperative, or the self-directed modes. Those who decide to keep the journal should be given a choice about whether and with whom they share journal entries. And they should be assured that they can make it what they wish. For some the journal will become primarily a detailed record of their professional experiences and their reactions to them: their reactions to books and journal articles; their responses to conferences and training sessions; their ideas for next week's lesson or next month's unit; their feelings about a supervisory interaction.

For others it will provide an opportunity for a more profound exploration of the meaning of their personal and professional lives. For such teachers a simple pattern like the following seems helpful:

Focus. Think about one encounter today that in retrospect seems important to you. Note in your journal the time and the place.

Recall. Recall the details of the experience: what was done, what was said, what was felt at the time. Try to recreate and thus re-live the experience. Write down all the details you can remember.

Reflect. Reflect about what the experience means to you now: what do you understand more clearly about your values, your culture, your teaching, your way of being in the world? Write about those understandings.

The goal here, of course, is to develop what Maxine Greene (1973) calls the disposition of being "critically attentive." Her words seem so apposite that they deserve to be quoted at length:

> *The teacher must probe, therefore, and try to understand what impinges on him in the everyday: the messages of the media; the impact of crowded streets; the atmosphere of shopping centers, government bureaus, schools; the privacy of his home. If he can write down some of what he perceives each day, so much the better. . . . Like his students, the teacher cannot help living much of the time in a world others prefabricate for what they consider to be the public. On occasion, he must be critically attentive; he must consciously choose what to appropriate and what to discard. Reliance on the natural attitude—a commonsense taking for granted of the everyday—will not suffice. In some fashion, the everyday must be rendered problematic so that questions may be posed (p. 11).*

To render the everyday life of teaching problematic—and in the process to develop the disposition of critical attentiveness: those are the goals of the reflective journal.

CHAPTER
7

Implementing the Differentiated System

The differentiated system of supervision is intended not only to give choices to the teachers; it is also designed to provide choices to the school or district. This chapter explains how those choices can be made and implemented, based on a decision-making and administrative process that has worked well in the pilot schools. Each district or school interested in using the program should, of course, vary these processes to suit local conditions.

Establishing Guidelines

The leadership team should meet together, after each member has had an opportunity to read this monograph or at least to become informed about the essential information. Ideally this meeting should occur in November or December prior to the school year in which the system will be implemented, in order to provide ample time for budgeting and scheduling requirements. Based on the team's assessment of the local context, the members should determine the broad guidelines within which the system must operate, answering the following questions:

1. If the decision is to be made at the district level, which schools will be involved?
2. Which individual will be primarily responsible for the administration of the program?

3. To what extent and in what manner will the teachers' association be consulted? Which contract provisions, if any, might influence the way the system operates?

4. What resources can be made available? In what ways and to what extent can funds and time be provided to support the program?

5. Are there any specific constraints that will govern the way the program should operate? Are there any district or school policies that will limit the options available to teachers?

Information and Input

If guidelines have been set at the district level, then the decision-making process now moves to the school level. The intent is to make this a school-based project, one for which school administrators and teachers feel a sense of ownership. Each school participating in the project should set up a project task force composed of administrators, supervisors, and teachers; a task force of five to six members seems to work best. The task force will have responsibility for planning, implementing, and evaluating the project. Task force members should read this monograph or a digest of its salient information, review the constraints previously established by the leadership team, and then develop a planning and implementation schedule.

At this time the task force should hold an information-and-input session for the faculty. The leader with primary responsibility for the project should introduce task force members, explain the function of the task force, specify the general goals of the project, review the rationale for a differentiated system, and clarify the guidelines previously established. It is also essential at this time to stress with the faculty that they will be actively involved in developing their own approach to differentiated supervision. This last point, perhaps, needs some elaboration and emphasis. I do not offer a monolithic model of differentiated supervision, which I want each school to implement in some pure form. I offer instead some options and ideas, based on sound research and tested in practice. My hope is that each school will develop its own differentiated system, which reflects the special insights of that faculty and responds to their special needs.

The program leader should then provide some basic information about the modes of supervision that will be made available to the faculty and should sketch in broad outline how the system might operate in that school. It is also essential at this point to be clear about the limits of teacher choice, so that there will be no confusion about this basic issue. Two points should probably be stressed. *First, every-one will be supervised in some fashion: "no supervision" is not an option. Second, the principal will retain veto power in the final deter-mination of who receives clinical supervision.* As noted in the previous chapter, research suggests that the cooperative and self-directed modes should be made available only to competent, experienced teachers. However, it is important to emphasize with the faculty that many experienced and competent teachers will choose clinical super-vision, simply because they value the professional growth that it provides. In this way those receiving clinical supervision are less likely to be stigmatized.

It is desirable for the leader to distribute a one- or two-page ques-tion-and-answer summary, which will help clarify possible misunder-standings and present the basic information in capsule form for any faculty members absent from the meeting. A sample question-and-an-swer summary for each mode of supervision is provided in the four appendices. They may be adapted for use by participating schools.

Program Planning

With the general parameters made clear and the basic information presented, the faculty should next meet in small groups, with a member of the task force leading each group. These small-group dis-cussions should be structured so that teachers have an opportunity to raise questions and share ideas. It is not a time to make decisions. The leader should then end this initial meeting by responding to the ques-tions raised in the small groups and by explaining the next steps in the decision-making process.

During the ensuing two or three weeks, the differentiated system should be discussed in-depth and explored in grade-level or de-partmental meetings, with a task force member present at each meet-ing to answer questions, note suggestions, and ascertain teachers' perceptions about the program. Our experience suggests that this stage should not be hurried; teachers will need time to digest the information, exchange ideas in a climate of openness, and reach some tentative decisions about how they want the system to operate.

Now the task force should re-convene to make specific decisions about the implementation of the program in that school. Figure 13 lists the important questions that should be answered before the system begins to operate. Perhaps some elaboration is needed here about the issue of which supervisory options will be offered. An essential

Figure 13. Implementation Issues

About the Differentiated System in General:
1. Who is responsible for administering the project?
2. What resources are available?
3. What supervisory options will be offered the teachers? Will teachers be limited to one mode—or may they choose to be involved in two of the modes? Will teachers be allowed to change their minds after the program is under way?
4. How will the project be monitored and evaluated?

About the Clinical Mode:
1. Which teachers will be required to receive clinical supervision?
2. Who will provide clinical supervision?
3. Will any particular approach to clinical supervision be used?
4. Are there any requirements about the number of observations and conferences to be held?
5. Will data from supervisory visits be used in the formal teacher evaluation program?

About Cooperative Professional Development:
1. Will teachers be encouraged to form cooperative teams within a grade level or subject field—or be given free choice about this issue?
2. How large will cooperative teams be?
3. What are the minimal expectations for each team? How many observations and conferences? Are any other cooperative activities expected?
4. Who will monitor the progress of the cooperative mode?
5. How will time be provided for observation and feedback?

About Self-Directed Development:
1. Who will serve as the primary resource for teachers who choose this mode?
2. To what extent will the goal-setting and self-assessment processes be formalized?
3. What are the minimal expectations for the number of conferences to be held?
4. What special resources are available for this component?
5. Who will monitor this mode?

About Administrative Monitoring:
1. Who will do the administrative monitoring?
2. Will administrative monitoring be required for all teachers—or offered as one of the options?
3. How will monitoring data be shared with teachers?
4. How will monitoring data be used in evaluating teachers?
5. Are there any minimal expectations about the length and frequency of monitoring visits?

principle of the differentiated system is that each school should decide how extensively it wishes to implement the several modes. There are basically four choices in resolving this issue:

- Use only administrative monitoring with clinical supervision. This is essentially a decision to formalize and improve what probably already exists.
- Use administrative monitoring, clinical supervision, and cooperative professional development.
- Use administrative monitoring, clinical supervision, and self-directed development.
- Use all four modes.

Each of these patterns was selected by one or more of the schools in the pilot studies—and each was successful in its own way.

It also should be noted that some schools have permitted teachers to be involved in two modes during one year. Initially, in developing the differentiated system, I assumed that every teacher would choose only one. However, in a number of the pilot schools, teachers said, "Why limit us to one choice? Some of us would like to have clinical supervision and cooperative development—or cooperative development and self-directed development." Allowing teachers to participate in more than one mode in a given year probably increases the administrative complexity of the program—but it makes sense to give teachers this option if they wish it.

With all these specific questions answered, the task force should convene a second faculty meeting to explain in detail how the program will operate at that school and to solicit teacher suggestions for further refinements. If the decisions made adequately reflect the faculty preferences and suggestions aired at previous meetings, then it is unlikely that major changes will be suggested; however, the opportunity for further modification should be provided.

Now the faculty is ready to be surveyed about their preferences. A brief form should be used, in which the basic limits (everyone is supervised; the principal has veto power) are restated and the options listed. After reviewing the results, the principal decides if any of the choices should be vetoed. I recommend to principals that they confer with each teacher whose choice is deemed unwise and convey somewhat directly a message to this effect: "I think that you and the school would profit if you had the benefits of some intensive clinical supervision." Some principals have been flexible here, indicating to the teacher that the decision will be reviewed at the end of the first semester.

Implementation and Evaluation

The program then gets under way, with each mode monitored by the individual responsible. After a few weeks into the project, a few teachers will ask if they can change to a different mode. Our experience in the pilot studies suggests that the best response here is to encourage teachers to stick with their first choice for at least two months—and then to permit teachers to make only one change at the end of that period. This practice seems to be a sensible middle ground between inflexibly saying, "No changes," and permissively letting teachers change their minds two or three times during a year.

Two summative assessment processes are suggested. First, all teachers in a given mode should meet together to openly discuss the strengths and weaknesses of that particular mode. The group leader, of course, should be responsible for recording reactions and reporting them to the project task force. Second, the entire faculty should be surveyed, using a form similar to the one shown in Figure 14.

The task force should review the results of the small-group discussions and the survey in recommending what should be done the following year. The schools we have worked with have made three different choices at this point. In one school the system worked so badly (largely because of administrator-faculty conflict) that the whole program was quietly laid to rest. In some schools, the faculty and administrators decided in essence to use the differentiated system every three or four years; in the intervening years, those schools used the basic combination of clinical supervision and administrative monitoring. One administrator put it this way: "The differentiated system worked well—it gave us a shot in the arm. But it takes time and effort. We'd like to put it on the back burner for a few years and then give it a fresh try—so that teachers don't get tired of it." And in a few schools the system worked so well that it has become a permanent part of the school's approach to the improvement of instruction.

So the differentiated system is not a panacea for all instructional ills. It will not work in every school. But, given the active support and cooperation of administrators, supervisors, and teachers, it can make a difference to those who are ready for a new form of professional growth.

Figure 14. Form for Evaluating the Differentiated System

Directions: We are interested in getting your candid reactions to the differentiated supervision system used in our school. Please answer the questions below.

1. Which supervisory mode were you involved in?

2. To what extent did you personally profit from your experience with this mode? (Check one)

_____ a great deal
_____ somewhat
_____ uncertain
_____ only a little
_____ not at all

3. To what extent do you believe the faculty in general profited from the differentiated system? (Check one)

_____ a great deal
_____ somewhat
_____ uncertain
_____ only a little
_____ not at all

4. What do you think was (were) the major strength(s) of the differentiated system?

_____

_____

5. In what ways do you think the differentiated system could be improved?

_____

_____

APPENDIX A

Overview of Clinical Supervision

Q. What is clinical supervision?

A. A systematic and carefully planned program of supervising a teacher, to assist the teacher to grow professionally. Typically, the clinical supervision process incorporates several cycles of pre-observation conference, observation, analysis of observational data, feedback conference, and evaluation of the cycle.

Q. How many such cycles are considered necessary?

A. The answer depends on the teacher's needs. While the issue has not been carefully researched, experience suggests that a minimum of five cycles is required to effect major improvement.

Q. Which teachers can profit from clinical supervision?

A. All teachers can profit from clinical supervision periodically in their careers. New teachers and teachers experiencing special problems in the classroom need it most of all.

Q. Who can provide clinical supervision?

A. It is best provided by someone who has had training and experience in the skills of planning, observing, analyzing, conferring, and evaluating. That individual might be an administrator, a supervisor, or an experienced teacher with special responsibilities and training.

Q. Should all teachers in a school receive clinical supervision?

A. As indicated above, all teachers can profit from the intensive assistance of clinical supervision. Even very experienced and competent teachers from time to time in their careers should have the benefits of clinical supervision. However, since clinical supervision to be effective requires a great deal of time, it seems reasonable to focus clinical efforts on teachers who request it or on those who the principal feels are especially in need of it.

Q. Will the observations made as part of the clinical supervision process be used also to rate or evaluate the teacher involved?

A. It seems desirable, in the opinion of most experts, to separate supervision and evaluation. Ordinarily, therefore, supervisory visits should not have an evaluative focus. However, the answer to this question is best determined by administrators and teachers consulting together under the guidance of district policy and developing an explicit agreement about the issue.

Q. What written records will be made of the clinical supervision?

A. Supervisors will probably keep two types of written records. First, many supervisors will keep a "clinical supervision log," which briefly notes the following: name of the teacher observed, class or period observed, date of observation, date and time when feedback conference was held, and a brief summary of the conference. This log is intended solely as a record for the supervisor.

Second, in addition to holding a feedback conference, the supervisor will probably give the teacher a written report, which includes the following: date and time of observation, class or period observed, chronological summary of important teaching and learning transactions, teaching strengths noted, and issues requiring discussion.

APPENDIX

B

Overview of Cooperative Professional Development

Q. What is cooperative professional development?

A. A process whereby a small group of teachers work together for their own improvement, observing each other's classes and conferring about those observations.

Q. How many observations and conferences are necessary?

A. A minimum of two cycles of pre-observation conferring, observing, and post-observational conferring is suggested. More would certainly be desirable.

Q. Which teachers can profit from cooperative professional development?

A. All teachers can profit from it. However, inexperienced teachers or teachers encountering special difficulties probably need the more intensive help of clinical supervision.

Q. How large should cooperative teams be?

A. Teams of two or three seem to work best.

Q. Which teachers should work together?

A. That's up to the principal and the teachers. Some teachers prefer to work with colleagues who have similar classes; others prefer to work with colleagues whose classes are quite different.

Q. *What can cooperative teams observe for?*

A. A colleague-observer can observe for whatever purpose the teacher to be observed requests: curriculum content, pupil behavior and learning, classroom climate and environment, instructional techniques. Observations will be more valuable if they have a definite focus.

Q. *What are the values of cooperative professional development?*

A. It enables teachers to become informed about what colleagues are doing. It gives teachers some new ideas that they can try in their own classrooms. It gives the person observed some objective feedback about teaching. It creates a professional climate and dialogue among teachers.

Q. *What is the role of the principal in cooperative professional development?*

A. To organize it, to get it going, and to monitor it occasionally just to be sure it is moving along in good fashion.

Q. *Are data from cooperative professional development made part of the evaluation process?*

A. Absolutely not.

Q. *What kinds of records should be kept of cooperative professional development?*

A. In order to monitor the program, the principal needs some record of what is happening. At the beginning the cooperative team submits a simple form outlining their plans; and at the end of the program they submit a second form summarizing what was accomplished. These are the only records necessary. As noted above, these reports should not include any data that might be used for evaluation purposes.

Suggestions for Holding a Cooperative Planning Conference

The classroom visit will probably be more productive if it is preceded by a brief planning conference. The following suggestions should be helpful.

1. Hold the planning conference at a time mutually agreeable and in a place where both parties can talk informally and freely.

2. Keep the conference relatively brief. Agree in advance about the general time limits so that both persons can make firm plans. Twenty minutes is usually enough time for the planning conference.

3. Agree about which class is to be observed. The teacher to be observed should give the colleague some background about the class and their progress. "This is a better-than-average group. Several of them seem just a bit unmotivated. We've been working on the term paper for the past few lessons."

4. The teacher who is to be observed should indicate briefly his or her plans for the class. "I'll begin by checking assignments. Then I plan to do some work on how to take notes from books and periodicals. I want them to learn how to make good notes without doing a lot of copying."

5. The teacher who is to be observed should be as specific as possible about the kind of feedback desired. Observations are more productive if they have a definite focus—and the teacher should determine that focus. The observer can focus on the teaching, the classroom environment, the curriculum, or the students. It's up to the teacher to decide. These matters are discussed more fully in the next section.

You can, of course, spend more time on the planning conference if you wish. Many teachers report that they have benefited most just by talking over their plans in detail with a colleague. A colleague can be a sounding board for their tentative ideas. They ask questions, share ideas, try out possible scenarios.

Possible Foci for Cooperative Observations

What should an observer look for when observing a class? The answer depends, of course, on the teacher's interests and professional needs.

In general, an observer can be asked to focus on four aspects of classroom interactions. We are now looking at the observation from the viewpoint of the teacher who is to be observed.

1. *The curriculum.* You can ask the observer to look mainly at your curriculum choices. Have you chosen content that seems at an appropriate level of difficulty? Does the content seem to be of interest to the

student? You ask the observer to look mainly at *what* you have chosen to teach, not how.

2. *The students.* You ask the observer to closely observe the students. You may ask the observer to look closely at one student who concerns you. Or there may be a group of students whom you feel you are not reaching. Or you may be interested in your general interactions with the class: Which students are you calling on? Which ones seem most involved? Which ones are inattentive? All this information would be important to you.

3. *General teaching techniques.* Several teaching skills seem generally effective in most subjects and across several grade levels. You can ask the observer to look closely at one of the following effective teaching skills or to give you objective feedback about your use of several of these skills.

Do you:

- Devote more time to teaching-learning activities and less time to classroom management?
- Set reasonably high expectations for students and make those expectations clear?
- Make clear to the students what they are expected to learn and how they may learn it?
- Increase the interest value of what is taught?
- Increase active student participation in the lesson and maintain a high degree of on-task student behavior?
- Give students a chance to apply and practice what they have learned?
- Give students frequent and appropriate feedback about their learning achievement and performance?
- Help students remedy learning deficiencies?
- Make fluid transitions between learning episodes?
- Maintain a classroom climate that is warm without being too friendly?

4. *Specific teaching techniques.* Some special teaching skills are more effective in particular subjects. In the teaching of writing, for example, providing pre-writing activities seems to be helpful to most students. The observer can look more closely at one of these skills, which you know to be effective in your subject or at your grade level.

It's also possible, of course, to ask the observer to just observe, without a predetermined focus. In such a case the observer will simply note all important teacher behaviors and student responses.

Suggestions for Making a Cooperative Observation

Below are some of the most commonly asked questions concerning the skills of making a classroom observation. Now we're looking at the observation from the observer's point of view.

Q. How long should I observe?

A. Stay for at least a half an hour. Try to see an entire learning episode, from beginning to end. At the secondary level your visit should probably last for the full period.

Q. Where do I sit?

A. The best place is in a spot where you can see both the teacher and the students' faces. But try to make yourself as unobtrusive as possible.

Q. Should I take notes?

A. You should probably make some form of record of what you see happening, unless the teacher being observed has asked you not to take notes. A great deal will go on in the classroom, and there will just be too much to remember.

Q. What notes do I take for an unfocused observation?

A. Make up your own form. Some observers simply keep a running account of what happens, noting the time in three- or five-minute increments. Another useful form uses four columns: time, teacher objectives, teacher activities, student responses.

Q. What notes do I take for a focused observation?

A. Here again the best answer is to devise your own simple form. Think about what the teacher has asked you to observe and rough out a form that will help you get the data you need. Suppose, for example, the teacher has asked you to look at student responses. With the teacher's cooperation make up a seating chart. Use your own easy-to-remember code to note such predictable behaviors as "volunteers answer," "does not answer when called on," and so on.

Suggestions for Holding a Cooperative Feedback Conference

After the observation the teacher who was observed and the observer meet for a feedback conference to discuss the observation. The following guidelines offer simple suggestions to make this conference productive.

1. The most important consideration is the tone of the conference: two professional colleagues are discussing a shared experience. The observer is not an evaluator making judgments. Neither is the observer a supervisor trying to bring about improvements in teaching. The observer is a colleague who was able to see what happened and can be of most help to the teacher by giving objective feedback and reflecting together with the teacher about what those data mean.

This tone can perhaps best be achieved if the teacher who was observed determines the agenda, asking questions of the observer, taking the lead in making sense of the data, and deciding when the conference ends. This tone of professionals sharing information can also be achieved if the teacher who was observed does not ask the observer to make judgments, by avoiding questions like, "What did you think of the lesson?"

2. What kinds of questions should the teacher ask the observer? If you asked for an unfocused or general observation, ask a question something like this: "What do you think was the most important thing going on that I might have missed?" Or a question like this is often useful: "I thought I had their interest until about half way through the period. Did you notice anything important at about that time?"

If you asked for a focused observation, then the questions are easier. Simply ask about the focus: "What did you notice about student responses?"

3. The observer should try to be as objective as possible, sharing information, not making judgments. There's nothing wrong with sincere praise, of course, but most of all the teacher wants specific information about what happened and why.

4. Keep the conference relatively brief—20 minutes should be enough. And try to hold it as soon after the observation as possible, while the details of the observation are still fresh in your mind.

C

Overview of Self-Directed Development

Q. What is self-directed development?

A. A process by which a teacher systematically plans for his or her own professional growth—and conscientiously carries out the plan over the course of a year.

Q. Which teachers can profit from self-directed development?

A. This component is probably most useful to teachers who meet three criteria: they are experienced and competent teachers; they are skilled in self-analysis and self-direction; and they prefer to work on their own, rather than with colleagues.

Q. What is the role of the principal in this component?

A. The principal serves mainly as a resource person: to help the teacher develop a plan for growth, to find the resources needed, and to assess progress.

Q. What are the values of self-directed development?

A. It probably helps the teacher become more insightful and more self-directing in achieving professional growth, and it facilitates a productive dialogue between the principal and the teacher.

Q. How can the teacher plan for self-directed development?

A. The teacher should have some flexibility here, since individual needs will vary so much. However, experience suggests that the program will be most profitable if the teacher prepares a written plan for self-directed development and discusses it with the principal. Typically, the plan will include these components: professional growth goal or goals for the year; the means by which the teacher hopes to achieve these goals (including readings, discussions, conferences, observations, tape recordings of classes); resources the teacher needs to achieve these goals (people, time, funds, equipment, materials); the way in which the teacher plans to assess progress; the kind of help the teacher requires from the principal.

Q. What is a professional growth goal?

A. A goal that the teacher hopes to achieve that year in his or her development as a teacher. Although it will always be concerned with some aspect of professional growth, it need not be directly related to the school system's stated goals—unless the district requires such a linkage. It provides a focus for the teacher's self-development efforts and aids the principal in providing the needed support. While the goal need not be quantifiable, it should be clear and unambiguous. Here are some examples of professional growth goals:

- To use the computer more efficiently in teaching problem solving.
- To learn about and implement cooperative learning strategies in my classroom.
- To develop and teach two new thematic units for my gifted pupils.

Q. Are data from self-directed development used in the evaluation process?

A. Only if the teacher wishes to have such data used. The teacher and the principal should make an explicit agreement about this matter. Ordinarily, self-appraisal is not sufficiently objective to be of central importance in the administrator's rating of the teaching.

Q. What records should be kept of the self-directed component?

A. As noted above, a written plan will probably facilitate the self-directed growth and will enable the principal to have some professional input. It will also be useful for both the teacher and the principal if the teacher prepares and shares a written self-assessment at the end of the year, although this assessment should probably be used only as a means of continuing the growth and the professional dialogue. As also noted above, the teacher's self-assessment should probably not be part of the administrator's rating of the teacher.

APPENDIX

D

Overview of Administrative Monitoring

Q. What is administrative monitoring?

A. Administrative monitoring is an informal process of briefly observing a class (or any supervised school activity) and giving the teacher some informal feedback about the observation. It is a process by which the principal maintains high visibility in the school, keeps in touch with school activities, makes on-the-spot assessments of learning, and demonstrates an active interest in all that is happening.

Q. Is it a substitute for clinical supervision?

A. No, because it lacks the systematic and intensive nature of such supervision.

Q. What are its values?

A. As noted above, it has several values. It gives the principal data about what is happening in the school. It demonstrates to teachers and pupils that the principal is actively concerned and involved. It enables the principal to monitor performance and to stay on top of problems. And it enables the principal to give teachers brief but frequent feedback about teaching and learning.

Q. How does the principal provide administrative monitoring?

A. By periodically making a tour of the school, stopping to visit a class for several minutes, noting significant data, and giving the teacher appropriate feedback.

Q. *Should all teachers be involved in administrative monitoring?*

A. All teachers should be involved in some manner, since all are part of the school and its programs. However, the principal may wish to provide *only* administrative monitoring for experienced and competent teachers who do not need clinical supervision and do not wish to be involved in one of the supervisory options.

Q. *Are observations made as part of administrative monitoring included in the evaluation process?*

A. Such informal observations can contribute to the evaluation process; however, they are not a substitute for systematic evaluative visits. The principal should be explicit with the teachers about the relationship of administrative monitoring to evaluation.

Q. *What records should be kept of administrative monitoring?*

A. It is recommended that the principal keep a written anecdotal record of any teacher behavior that merits commendation or indicates improvement is needed. The record should note the date, time, and place of the observation and record briefly the behavior involved. This anecdotal record should be available for the teacher to examine at any time.

In addition, the principal may wish to keep a record of the dates and hours of all monitoring, solely for administrative purposes.

References

Acheson, K. A., and Gall, M. D. *Techniques in the Clinical Supervision of Teachers: Preservice and Inservice Application.* New York: Longman, 1980.

Aleamoni, L. M. "The Usefulness of Student Evaluations in Improving College Teaching." *Instructional Science* 7 (January 1978): 95–105.

Aleamoni, L. M. "Student Ratings of Instruction." In *Handbook of Teacher Evaluation,* pp. 110–145. Edited by J. Millman. Beverly Hills, Calif.: Sage, 1981.

Alfonso, R. J. "Will Peer Supervision Work?" *Educational Leadership* 34 (May 1977): 594–601.

Alfonso, R. J.; Firth, G. R.; and Neville, R. F. *Instructional Supervision: A Behavior System.* Boston: Allyn and Bacon, 1981.

Alfonso, R. J.; and Goldsberry, L. "Colleagueship in Supervision." In *Supervision of Teaching,* pp. 90–107. Edited by T. J. Sergiovanni. Alexandria, Va.: Association for Supervision and Curriculum Development, 1982.

Anderson, G. J., and Walberg, H. J. "Learning Environments." In *Evaluating Educational Performance,* pp. 81–98. Edited by H. J. Walberg. Berkeley, Calif.: McCutchan, 1974.

Armstrong, H. R. "Performance Evaluation." *National Elementary Principal* 52 (February 1973): 51–55.

Ball, E. J. "Structuring a Differentiated Supervisory Program in an Independent School." Ph.D. dissertation, University of Pennsylvania, 1981.

Beck, J. S. "An Individualized Program of Supervision for Teachers of the Learning Disabled." Ph.D. dissertation, University of Pennsylvania, 1982.

Bents, R. H., and Howey, K. R. "Staff Development: Change in the Individual." In *Staff Development/Organization Development,* pp. 11–36. Edited by B. Dillon-Peterson. Alexandria, Va.: Association for Supervision and Curriculum Development, 1981.

Berman, P., and McLaughlin, M. *Federal Programs Supporting Educational Change.* Vol. 8: *Implementing and Sustaining Innovations.* Santa Monica, Calif.: Rand Corporation, 1978.

Blumberg, A. *Supervisors and Teachers: A Private Cold War.* 2nd ed. Berkeley, Calif.: McCutchan, 1980.

Brophy, J. E. *Using Observations to Improve Your Teaching.* East Lansing, Mich.: Institute for Research on Teaching, 1979.

Bryan, R. C. "The Teacher's Image Is Stubbornly Stable." *Clearing House* 40 (April 1966): 459–460.

Calfee, R. "Cognitive Psychology and Educational Practice." In *Review of Research in Education 9,* pp. 3–74. Edited by D. C. Berliner. Washington, D.C.: American Educational Research Association, 1981.

Carroll, J. G. "Faculty Self-Evaluation." In *Handbook of Teacher Evaluation,* pp. 180–200. Edited by J. Millman. Beverly Hills, Calif.: Sage, 1981.

Cawelti, G., and Reavis, C. "How Well Are We Providing Instructional Improvement Services?" *Educational Leadership* 38 (December 1980): 236–240.

Chalker, J. "A Field Test of the Feasibility of Implementing a Differentiated System of Supervision and Evaluation in a Selected Suburban High School." Ph.D. dissertation, University of Pennsylvania, 1979.

Cogan, M. L. *Clinical Supervision.* Boston: Houghton Mifflin, 1973.

Cooper, G. "Collegial Supervision: The Feasibility of Implementation and Particular Effectiveness on Teacher Attitudes and Job Satisfaction." Ph.D. dissertation, University of Pennsylvania, 1983.

Copeland, W. D. "Affective Disposition of Teachers in Training toward Examples of Supervisory Behavior." *Journal of Educational Research* 74 (September-October 1980): 37–42.

Eaker, R. E. "An Analysis of the Clinical Supervision Process as Perceived by Selected Teachers and Administrators." Ph.D. dissertation, University of Tennessee, 1972.

Edwards, C. H. "Changing Teacher Behavior through Self Instruction and Supervised Micro Teaching in a Competency Based Program." *Journal of Educational Research* 68 (February 1975): 219–222.

Eisner, E. W. *The Educational Imagination.* New York: Macmillan, 1979.

Eisner, E. W. "An Artistic Approach to Supervision." In *Supervision of Teaching*, pp. 53–66. Edited by T. J. Sergiovanni. Alexandria, Va.: Association for Supervision and Curriculum Development, 1982.

Fenstermacher, G. D. "A Philosophical Consideration of Recent Research in Teacher Effectiveness." In *Review of Research in Education 6*, pp. 157–186. Edited by D. C. Berliner. Washington, D.C.: American Educational Research Association, 1978.

Freeman, G.; Palmer, R. C.; and Ferren, A. S. "Team Building for Supervisory Support." *Educational Leadership* 37 (January 1980): 356–358.

Fuller, F. F., and Manning, B. A. "Self-Confrontation Reviewed: A Conceptualization for Video Playback in Teacher Education." *Review of Educational Research* 43 (Fall 1973): 469–528.

Garman, N. B. "A Study of Clinical Supervision as a Resource of College Teachers of English." Ph.D. dissertation, University of Pittsburgh, 1971.

Glickman, C. D. *Developmental Supervision: Alternative Practices for Helping Teachers Improve Instruction.* Alexandria, Va.: Association for Supervision and Curriculum Development, 1981.

Goldhammer, R. *Clinical Supervision: Special Methods for the Supervision of Teachers.* New York: Holt, Rinehart, and Winston, 1969.

Good, T., and Brophy, J. *Looking in Classrooms.* 2nd ed. New York: Harper and Row, 1978.

Gordon, B. "Teachers Evaluate Supervisory Behavior in the Individual Conference." *Clearing House* 49 (January 1976): 231–238.

Gray, F., and Burns, M. L. "Does 'Management by Objectives' Work in Education?" *Educational Leadership* 36 (March 1979): 414–417.

Greene, M. *Teacher as Stranger: Educational Philosophy for the Modern Age.* Belmont, Calif.: Wadsworth, 1973.

Harris, B. N. *Supervisory Behavior in Education.* 2nd ed. Englewood Cliffs, N.J.: Prentice-Hall, 1975.

Holdaway, E. A., and Millikan, R. A. "Educational Consultation: A Summary of Four Alberta Studies." *Alberta Journal of Educational Research* 26 (September 1980): 194–210.

Hook, C. M., and Rosenshine, B. "Accuracy of Teacher Reports of Their Teaching Behavior." *Review of Educational Research* 49 (Winter 1979): 1–12.

Iwanicki, E. F. "Contract Plans: A Professional Growth-Oriented Approach to Evaluating Teacher Performance." In *Handbook of Teacher Evaluation*, pp. 203–228. Edited by J. Millman. Beverly Hills, Calif.: Sage, 1981.

Joyce, B., and McKibbin, M. "Teacher Growth States and School Environments." *Educational Leadership* 40 (November 1982): 36–41.

Joyce, B., and Weil, M. *Models of Teaching.* 2nd ed. Englewood Cliffs, N.J.: Prentice-Hall, 1980.

Kerman, S. "Teacher Expectations and Student Achievement." *Phi Delta Kappan* 6 (June 1979): 716–718.

Kerr, B. J. "An Investigation of the Process of Using Feedback Data Within the Clinical Supervision Cycle to Facilitate Teachers Individualization of Instruction." Ph.D. dissertation, University of Pittsburgh, 1976.

Knowles, M. *The Adult Learner: A Neglected Species*. Houston: Gulf, 1978.

Krajewski, R. J. "Clinical Supervision: To Facilitate Teacher Self-Improvement." *Journal of Research and Development In Education* 9 (Winter 1976): 58–66.

Kulik, C. L.; Kulik, J. A.; and Cohen, P. A. "Instructional Technology and College Teaching." *Teaching of Psychology* 7 (December 1980): 199–205.

Lawrence, G. *Patterns of Effective Inservice Education: A State of the Art Summary of Research on Materials and Procedures for Changing Teacher Behaviors in Inservice Education*. ERIC Document Reproduction Service, ED 176 424, 1974.

Lawrence, G., and Branch, J. "Peer Support as the Heart of Inservice Education." *Theory Into Practice* 17 (June 1978): 245–247.

Leithwood, K. A., and Montgomery, D. J. "The Role of the Elementary Principal in Program Improvement." *Review of Educational Research* 52 (Fall 1982): 309–339.

Lewis, J. *Appraising Teacher Performance*. West Nyack, N.Y.: Parker, 1973.

Lieberman, M. "Should Teachers Evaluate Other Teachers?" *School Management* 16 (June 1972): 4–6.

Little, J. W. "Norms of Collegiality and Experimentation: Workplace Conditions of School Success." *American Educational Research Journal* 19 (Fall 1982): 325–340.

Lovell, J. T., and Phelps, M. S. "Supervision in Tennessee: A Study of Perceptions of Teachers, Principals, and Supervisors." Murfreesboro, Tenn.: Tennessee Association for Supervision and Curriculum Development, 1976.

McGreal, T. L. *Successful Teacher Evaluation*. Alexandria, Va.: Association for Supervision and Curriculum Development, 1983.

McGuire, G. K.; Borth, A. M.; Pudendorf, I. E.; and Rose, J. P. "Visiting Other Teachers in Your School: A Basis for Communication." *The Elementary School Journal* 58 (March 1958): 331–334.

McKeachie, W. J. "Student Ratings of Faculty: A Reprise." *Academe* 65 (October 1979): 384–397.

McNeil, J. D. *Toward Accountable Teaching*. New York: Holt, Rinehart, and Winston, 1971.

McNeil, J. D. "A Scientific Approach to Supervision." In *Supervision of Teaching*, pp. 18–34. Edited by T. J. Sergiovanni. Alexandria, Va.: Association for Supervision and Curriculum Development, 1982.

McNeil, J. D., and Popham, W. J. "The Assessment of Teacher Competence." In *Second Handbook of Research on Teaching*, pp. 218–244. Edited by M. W. Travers. Chicago: Rand McNally, 1973.

Medley, D. M. "The Effectiveness of Teachers." In *Research on Teaching*, pp. 11–27. Edited by P. L. Peterson and H. J. Walberg. Berkeley, Calif.: McCutchan, 1979.

Minton, E. "Clinical Supervision: Developing Evaluation Skills for Dynamic Leadership." 1982. (Mimeographed.)

Moritz, W., and Martin-Reynolds, J. A. "Split-Screen Video Taping: The Genie in the Bottle." *Educational Leadership* 38 (February 1980): 396–399.

Muir, L. L. "The Rationale, Design, Implementation, and Assessment of a Peer Supervision Program for Elementary Schools." Ph.D. dissertation, University of Pittsburgh, 1980.

Nelson, J.; Schwartz, M.; and Schmuck, R. *Collegial Supervision: A Sub-study of Organization Development in Multi-Unit Schools*. Bethesda, Md.: ERIC Document Reproduction Service, ED 166 841, 1974.

Perrone, V. *Documentation: A Process for Classroom/Program Evaluation and Personal/ Professional Learning*. Grand Forks, N.D.: Center of Teaching and Learning, 1977.

Peterson, P. L. "Direct Instruction Reconsidered." In *Research on Teaching*, pp. 57–69. Edited by H. J. Walberg. Berkeley, Calif.: McCutchan, 1979.

Reavis, C. A. "A Test of the Clinical Supervision Model." *Journal of Educational Research* 70 (July-August 1977): 311–315.

Redfern, G. B. *Evaluating Teachers and Administrators: A Performance Objectives Model.* Boulder, Colo.: Westview, 1980.

Ritz, W. C., and Cashell, J. G. " 'Cold War' Between Supervisors and Teachers?" *Educational Leadership* 38 (October 1980): 77–78.

Russell, D., and Hunter, M. *Planning for Effective Instruction* Los Angeles: University Elementary School, 1980.

Ryan, K. *The Teacher's Story: The Oldest and Newest Form of Educational Research.* Bethesda, Md.: ERIC Document Reproduction Service, ED 208 597, 1981.

Santmire, T. E. "Developmental Differences in Adult Learners: Implications for Staff Development." Position paper, 1979.

Sergiovanni, T. J. "Toward a Theory of Supervisory Practice: Integrating Scientific, Clinical, and Artistic Views." In *Supervision of Teaching*, pp. 67–78. Edited by T. J. Sergiovanni. Alexandria, Va.: Association for Supervision and Curriculum Development, 1982.

Shapiro, J. "A Feasibility Study of a Differentiated Supervision and Evaluation Model for Teachers." Ph.D. dissertation, University of Pennsylvania, 1978.

Shaw, J. S. "Students Evaluate Teachers and (Better Sit Down) It Works." *Nation's Schools* 91 (April 1973): 49–53.

Shields, C. R. "A Feasibility Study of Differentiated Supervision for Catholic Schools." Ph.D. dissertation, University of Pennsylvania, 1982.

Shinn, J. L. "Teacher Perceptions of Ideal and Actual Supervisory Procedures Used by California Elementary Principals: The Effects of Supervisory Training Programs Sponsored by the Association of California School Administrators." Ph.D. dissertation, University of Oregon, 1976.

Shuma, K. Y. "Changes Effectuated by a Clinical Supervisory Relationship Which Emphasize a Helping Relationship and a Conference Format Made Congruent with the Establishment and Maintenance of This Helping Relationship." Ph.D. dissertation, University of Pittsburgh, 1973.

Smithman, H. H., and Lucio, W. H. "Supervision by Objectives: Pupil Achievement as a Measurement of Teacher Performance." *Educational Leadership* 31 (January 1974): 338–344.

Squires, D. A.; Huitt, W. G.; and Segars, J. K. "Improving Classrooms and Schools: What's Important." *Educational Leadership:* 39 (December 1981): 174–179.

Sturges, A. W.; Krajewski, R. J.; Lovell, J. T.; McNeill, E.; and Ness, M. G. *The Roles and Responsibilities of Instructional Supervisors.* Alexandria, Va.: Association for Supervision and Curriculum Development, 1978.

Sullivan, C. G. *Clinical Supervision: A State of the Art Review.* Alexandria, Va.: Association for Supervision and Curriculum Development, 1980.

Sullivan, C. G. "Supervisory Expectations and Work Realities: The Great Gulf." *Educational Leadership* 39 (March 1982): 448–451.

Withall, H., and Wood, F. H. "Taking the Threat Out of Classroom Observation and Feedback." *Journal of Teacher Education* 30 (January-February 1979): 55–58.

Yinger, R. J., and Clark, C. M. *Reflective Journal Writing: Theory and Practice.* East Lansing, Mich.: Institute for Research on Teaching, 1981.

Young, J. M., and Heichberger, R. L. "Teacher Perceptions of an Effective School Supervision and Evaluation Program." *Education* 96 (Fall 1975): 10–19.

For supervisors, administrators, and
students of supervision —

Readings in Educational Supervision

From <u>Educational Leadership</u>

This special ASCD edition of 42 articles covers important
topics on educational supervision published in
Educational Leadership in recent years.

Editors Edith E. Grimsley and Ray E. Bruce of the University of Georgia have
compiled works by such respected writers as Thomas Sergiovanni, Madeline
Hunter, Ben Harris, Allan Glatthorn, Fenwick English, A.W. Sturges, Carl
Glickman, and many others.

Each article falls into one of the nine topic areas most frequently addressed
by writers of textbooks on educational supervision and by instructors, including:

- The history, nature, purposes, and tasks of educational supervision
- Trends in organization for supervisory services
- Human skills in supervision
- Supervisory techniques for planning and managing educational programs
- The supervisor as facilitator in the improvement of teaching and learning
- The supervisor as leader in curriculum and staff development
- The supervisor as a researcher and member of the profession

Readings in Educational Supervision brings together in one volume
articles of lasting value to leaders seriously concerned with improving
instruction, including:

- Six Types of Supervisory Conferences, **Madeline Hunter**
- Clinical Supervision in the 1980s, **Karolyn J. Snyder**
- Shared Leadership — "The Damn Thing Works," **David Weingast**
- A Concerns-Based Approach to Curriculum Change, **Susan Loucks and Harold Pratt**
- Guidelines for Better Staff Development, **Fred H. Wood and Steven R. Thompson**
- The Developmental Approach to Supervision, **Carl D. Glickman**

Stock Number: 611-82272. 201 pp. $9.00.
To order, complete and mail the order form that follows.

Other ASCD Publications on Supervision

BOOKS

Successful Teacher Evaluation   Thomas L. McGreal
Describes eight common characteristics of teacher evaluation systems
that have proven effective in existing school districts, and discusses the
development and implementation of new evaluation systems.
Stock Number: 611-83300. 161 pp. $8.75.

MEDIA

Evaluating Teacher Performance: Part I. The Process.
Richard Manatt explains a valid, reliable, and legal way to assess
teacher performance using generic instruments (included) and
performance analysis. He leads viewers through the process of
evaluating four real elementary and secondary teaching episodes.
60 min. Member, $195; Nonmember, $230.

Evaluating Teacher Performance: Part II. Teaching Episodes.
Consists of three more teaching episodes plus longer versions of two
segments of Part I, including third grade reading, secondary industrial
arts, sixth grade social studies, first grade reading, and secondary art.
60 min. Member, $195; Nonmember, $230.

Supervising the Marginal Teacher
Designed to guide school administrators through especially difficult
phases of the teacher perfomance evaluation process. Richard Manatt
describes the use of intensive assistance, progressive discipline, and
teacher dismissal, and advises a principal in the implementation of
these strategies. Packaged with a comprehensive leader's guide and
instructional materials booklet.
60 min. Member, $225; Nonmember, $260.

**The Supervisory Process: Helping Teachers to Improve
Instruction.**
Demonstrates a practical way for supervisors to work directly with
teachers to improve instruction. A teacher and principal simulate the five
stages of this process, which is based on the clinical supervision model:
the Pre-Observation Conference, the Observation, Analysis and
Strategy, the Post-Observation Conference, and the Post-Conference
Analysis. This program is designed to involve the viewer and to
encourage any persons in a department, team, or school who wish to
work together to improve instructional supervisory practices.
30 min. Member, $195; Nonmember, $230.

ORDER FORM

BOOKS

Title	Stock Number	Quantity	Cost per Item	Total Cost
Readings in Educational Supervision	611-82272		$9.00	
Successful Teacher Evaluation	611-83300		$8.75	

MEDIA

Title	Format*	No. of Copies	Cost — Member	Cost — Nonmember	Rental Cost $50.	Preview Cost $30.	Total Cost
Evaluating Teacher Performance: Part I. The Process			$195.	$230.			
Evaluating Teacher Performance: Part II. Teaching Episodes			$195.	$230.			
Supervising the Marginal Teacher			$195.	$230.			
The Supervisory Process: Helping Teachers to Improve Instruction			$195.	$230.			

*Available (¾ Cassette, ½ Beta, or ½ VHS)

Ordering Information

Complete form and mail to:

ASCD

Association for Supervision and Curriculum Development
Department 1149
225 North Washington Street,
Alexandria, VA 22314

Please check form of payment:

☐ Enclosed is my check or money order in the amount of $ _____ . (If payment is enclosed, ASCD absorbs cost of postage and handling.)

☐ Bill me. (Postage and handling extra. Orders from institutions and businesses must be on an official purchase order form.)

Payment must accompany orders under $20.

_____
NAME

_____
STREET

_____
CITY   STATE   ZIP

(____) _____
TELEPHONE